AROUND THE WORLD IN FORTY YEARS

AROUND THE WORLD IN FORTY YEARS

Andy Moles

with Geoffrey Dean

forewords by Tim Munton and Gladstone Small

FAIRFIELD BOOKS

First published by Fairfield Books in June 2025

fairfield books

Fairfield Books
Bedser Stand
Kia Oval
London
SE11 5SS

The right of Andy Moles to be identified as the author of this work
has been asserted by him in accordance with sections 77 and 78
of the Copyright, Designs and Patents Act 1988

This book is printed on paper certified
by the Forest Stewardship Council

Every effort has been made to trace copyright and any oversight
will be rectified in future editions at the earliest opportunity

All rights reserved. No part of this book may be reproduced, sold, utilised
or transmitted in any form or by any electronic or mechanical means,
including photocopying, recording or by any information storage and
retrieval system, without prior permission in writing from the publishers

The views and opinions expressed in this book are those of the
author and do not necessarily reflect the views of the publishers

© Andy Moles and Geoffrey Dean
ISBN 978-1-915237-64-4

A CIP catalogue record for this title is available from the British Library

Printed by CPI Group (UK) Ltd

CONTENTS

	Acknowledgements	7
	Foreword by Gladstone Small	9
	Foreword by Tim Munton	11
	Tribute by Tony Finch	17
	Prologue	19
1	Early years and Warwickshire debut	21
2	Griqualand West and county cap	34
3	Wedding and a final winter playing in South Africa	41
4	A first trophy	43
5	1990 – a record year	46
6	My approach to batting	48
7	Improvement under Bob Woolmer	51
8	1994 – the treble-winning year	56
	Tribute by Brian Lara	66
9	1995 – league and cup double	67
10	Tales from the county circuit	70
	Tribute by Allan Donald	81
11	Free State and Hansie Cronje	82
12	Kenya	92
13	Scotland	97
14	New Zealand	105
	Tributes by Andrew Strauss & Kane Williamson	126
15	Reviving my love for the game	128
16	Afghanistan	131
	Tribute by Naveen-ul-Haq	144
17	Living in Kabul	145
18	Amputation	151
	Tribute by Brand van den Heever	162
19	Uzbekistan	164
20	The Bahamas	167
21	Blessed by family	169
	Career statistics	170
	Index	174

Acknowledgements

This book is dedicated to my two sons, Daniel and Matthew. You continue to inspire me every day.

The book would not have got off the ground without the hard work from Geoffrey Dean, my ghost writer, and Matt Thacker, my publisher. Thank you. Credit as well to Stephen Chalke, for editing the manuscript.

Special thanks go to five friends who have supported me in getting the book to print: Tony Finch, Mark Farrelly, Gary Pettet, Simon Millington and Martin Curd.

I'm also very grateful for the twin forewords from Tim Munton and Gladstone Small, as well as the tributes from Allan Donald, Tony Finch, Brand van den Heever, Brian Lara, Naveen-ul-Haq, Andrew Strauss and Kane Williamson.

Last but not least, a huge thankyou to all the team-mates and players that I have had the privilege of sharing a dressing room with for over forty years.

Moler

Foreword

Gladstone Small

Warwickshire & England cricketer

There are people you meet in life who leave a lasting impact – those whose journeys inspire, whose resilience motivates and whose friendship becomes a cornerstone of your own story. Andy Moles is one of these people for me. We were more than just team-mates; we were brothers on and off the field, sharing victories, defeats and moments that shaped us both.

Through the years I've watched him face challenges with a strength and determination that is nothing short of remarkable. Whether it was in competition or in life's toughest moments, he never backed down. I always wanted him in my corner. He was a team-mate who would fight to the very end. His story isn't just about personal triumph; it's a testament to perseverance, loyalty and the power of never giving up.

What makes this book special is that it's not just a recollection of events. It's a journey through the highs and lows that made him who he is today. His words carry the weight of experience, the wisdom of reflection and the passion of someone who truly understands what it means to push forward.

Some of my fondest memories with him extend far beyond the field: bar drinks that stretched into late-night curries, countless rounds on the golf course and the unshakeable camaraderie that defined our time together. I loved watching that bristling walk out to bat, knowing he was about to take on the new ball with gutsy termination, a skilled, stubborn defence and a mix of stroke play that silenced bowlers who dared to intimidate. Forget about bowlers sledging him – Moler got his jibes in first.

One unforgettable moment was the 1993 NatWest final that saw a famous Bears victory. Neither of us covered ourselves in glory on the field that day, but we made sure we were the last ones to leave the Lord's dressing-rooms, having ensured that every last drop of any alcoholic beverages was fully consumed.

For those who know him, this book will reinforce everything we admire about him. And for those who don't, you're about to meet someone whose story will stay with you long after you turn the last page. I'm honoured to introduce this book, just as I've been honoured to call Moler a team-mate and a friend. His story deserves to be told, and I have no doubt it will inspire everyone who reads it.

Foreword

Tim Munton

Warwickshire & England cricketer

Moler and I were brought together as team-mates at Warwickshire in 1986, when we both broke into the first team. Our great friendship was spawned when we became 'roomies' in Bristol the week after Moler's championship debut at Old Trafford in early June. Both of us were apt to snore, and David Brown, the Warwickshire manager, impolitely informed us that, after representations by other team-mates, the only option was to pair us together on away trips.

There began a friendship that went beyond our wildest dreams. We've had each other's backs since that 1986 season 39 years ago. Late-night feasts of crisps, biscuits and chocolate bars, having driven from Hove to Old Trafford or Essex to Headingley, through to great stories of battles shared and successes achieved, on the field over pints of hand-pulled Tetley and Brian's Fish & Chips in Leeds to local ale and 'The Hottest Curry' in Darlington. Our friendship off the field has also given us many shared special family moments: with our kids, Millie & Harry and Danny & Matthew, growing up together around county cricket grounds in the 1980s and '90s – including a very special memory shared when in 1992 Andy waited at the QE Hospital in Birmingham to drive me at midnight down to Gatwick Airport after the birth of my son Harry that evening, to board the flight the following morning for the England 'A Team' tour of Bermuda and the Caribbean. How different things are today!

One of my fondest and lasting memories of our lives together is when he and our mutual GREAT friend Tony Finch ('Finchy') were joint best men when I married Sonia. One of my favourite photos of all time is of the three of us together on the wedding day.

Andy's career has been, and still is, 'Hard Fought' all the way. From finally joining the Warwickshire staff at the age of 25 as a player, and it's only when you look back at his record you appreciate what a VERY fine opening bat he was, and to this day an excellent coach, with a real ability to develop young emerging talent into fine first-class and international cricketers. He's one of very few English batsmen with a career average of over 40 not to play for England and a key member of the Warwickshire team from 1986 to 1996, winning seven trophies along the way. His CV from his coaching career is also littered with successes: coaching Orange Free State in South Africa to a plate trophy and Northern Districts in New Zealand to the domestic championship title there; getting Scotland to the 2007 World Cup in the West Indies as the top associate country qualifier; coach of New Zealand at the ICC Champions Trophy Final in 2009; and coach of Afghanistan when they reached the World Cup in Australia and New Zealand in 2015. For him, and me, a real sadness is that he never had the opportunity to coach in England, and particularly his beloved Warwickshire. It is something he's at peace with now but has left a major gap in a career littered with success away from his home county.

I'm blessed to have shared so many of my fondest memories in life with Andy. Most of the ones on the field you will either know or read about in the pages that follow. I've picked three less well-known memories that typify the hard-working, passionate, gutsy and aggressive guy I'm privileged to have as my friend, never taking a step back on or off the field. He is stubborn, principled and loyal in sport, and life, to a fault. The three stories highlight the unique nature of our friendship that has endured despite Andy's career and life playing out away from the UK.

Leaving New Zealand
The first story illustrates how relationships with cricketing team-mates are generally so special, and endure in spite of distance and years without contact. Some of Moler's most successful years as a coach were in, and with, New Zealand. Having led Northern Districts to the New Zealand domestic championship, Andy was appointed as head coach of the New Zealand national team. For a while, this was a perfect match for Moler: coaching a side full of talent that was often under-appreciated but thrived on being the underdog. Having reached the final of the Champions Trophy in 2009, you would have thought

future success was not far away. Therefore I was surprised to receive a phone call in November 2009 (noon in NZ; 11pm in the UK) from Andy to tell me he'd just come out of a meeting with NZ Cricket where he was told his services were no longer required.

Clearly stunned, disappointed and angry, he shared a version of events that sounded unjust, to say the least. We chatted for the best part of an hour about what his next steps should be to counter something that, reputationally and financially, could be very damaging. Clearly a good legal counsel was going to be important. Mid-way through our telephone call, I had a flashback to someone who had been incredibly good and supportive of me some 24 years earlier. I had my first overseas cricketing winter away from home, playing and coaching in Wellington, New Zealand. A recently qualified lawyer, Mark Freeman, was my flatmate and opening bowling partner at Victoria University, Wellington. I remembered Mark to be a talented cricketer, but in the context of our call I recalled he also seemed to be on course for a successful career in law. With no contact since the spring of 1986, I googled 'Mark Freeman, Lawyer, New Zealand'. Surprisingly and very fortunately, Mark's career had progressed to him being a partner in one of New Zealand's leading law firms. The website of the law firm in Auckland had his mobile number, which I called straight away, and he answered immediately. Naturally the call started with me introducing myself: "Hi, Mark, Tim Munton here." His response was friendly but to the point: "Great to hear from you, Tim, but after 23 years without contact, how can I help you?" Suffice to say the detail thereafter isn't for sharing, other than that one of his colleagues was a great help in getting a satisfactory outcome for Andy very soon after.

The Most Dangerous Job in Cricket
After losing his job with New Zealand Andy had a good few months reflecting on his next steps, taking a few short-term roles before being approached by the Afghanistan cricket team where he held a number of key positions over a five-and-a-half-year period. The highlight must have been coaching them at the Cricket World Cup in 2015.

I remember when Andy first called to tell me he had been offered the job to coach Afghanistan. I was obviously pleased he'd been offered another top job in the game but naturally concerned when he told me he was going to be spending time in Kabul. It was a particularly turbulent time in the country, with westerners strongly advised not to visit. Andy's approach was typical of his character: "If I take the job I have to spend time in the country and meet the people involved in cricket." During his first stint over there he was based in a heavily protected hotel where the western media and dignitaries were based. He shared security briefings where he was told where to sit in restaurants to minimise the impact of bombings at the hotel or where to position yourself for a quick exit in the event of attack by gunmen. During this time we spoke most days, and typically of him most of the conversation was about the amazing young talent in the country, with only passing comments about the violence and risks he faced every day travelling from the hotel to cricket training.

During his second stint with Afghanistan I asked how he was getting on, to which he replied: "The budgets didn't stretch to the secure hotel this time, I'm staying above the clubhouse at the training ground." Blindly brave and driven, Andy chose to visit and stay in Kabul with no security, believing that nobody would be looking to do harm to the national coach of the cricket team. The Taliban apparently liked cricket, so he was in more danger of being caught in crossfire or streetside bombs, while travelling to and from the hotel, than he was of being targeted at the cricket ground. He had several happy years in coaching and high performance roles with Afghanistan, being somewhat oblivious to the fact he was actually in 'The Most Dangerous Job in Cricket'.

I am officially your short leg
Bizarrely and tragically it wasn't a gun or a bomb that impacted Andy's life during his time in Afghanistan. It was an MRSA infection in his foot.

During a training camp at the ICC's training facilities in Abu Dhabi, he decided, as Andy and I often do, that he needed to lose some weight and get fit. He set out on a two-hour 'power walk' in the middle of the afternoon in Abu Dhabi in 40 degree plus heat. At the end of the walk he noticed he had a blister on the sole of his left foot. Not any old blister but one that covered the hole of his foot and was very deep.

The physio and medical team were concerned, and I'd get updates two or three times a week with photographic evidence showing the slow but steady recovery during the subsequent six-week training camp in India. The camp came to an end in February 2020 just as COVID was becoming a thing around the world, and Andy headed home to Cape Town, South Africa. My last call before his departure from India brought good news and a picture showing that the wound in his foot was all but healed. There was, though, a cautionary note to say there were signs of an infection in his little toe, and the physio had insisted he go straight to the hospital when he arrived in Cape Town to have it checked out.

What followed over the following weeks was nothing short of devastating for Andy. The germ turned out to be an MRSA infection that spread throughout his foot. There were numerous attempts to save it by amputating first his little toe, then more significant parts of his foot. Then came the life-changing call for the man I'm lucky to call my best friend. We were in touch early that particular morning as he had an early appointment at the hospital with the consultant in Cape Town. He wasn't sure what time the consultant was going to see him, so I went for a shower. When I returned to my bedroom I could see a message on my phone. It was from Andy, and all he said was: "H (my Warwickshire nickname), I am Officially Your Short Leg."

Of course I knew what the message meant, and I couldn't believe that, even with such dark news, Moler was thinking of others and how best to share the revelation with least impact and with humour. It was, though, the phone call ten minutes later that really defined the man, when he shared the detail of the conversation with his consultant. The consultant had explained that, despite the intervention of the most powerful antibiotics and increasingly severe amputation of parts of his foot, the infection was as rampant as ever. The medical staff were concerned he might lose the whole of his leg and possibly his life if they didn't quickly do something more radical. His recommendation was to amputate the leg just below the knee, believing this would get ahead of the path of the infection up his leg.

Clearly, this was not an easy thing to come to terms with, and I'd be wrong to say the past five years have been plain sailing for Andy, but my goodness has he demonstrated all of those character traits I mentioned at the start of this foreword. As a great friend of Moler, I'd like to acknowledge and thank the skill, commitment and decisive action of the medical team in Cape Town and the friendship and support of so many of his friends in cricket. In particular, thanks must also go to the Cricketers' Trust and the team at the PCA for their help and support when he truly needed it.

Moler, I'm so pleased that you decided to write this book with Geoffrey Dean, and I know it's only been made possible through the support of a group of other very special friends of yours. It is a real honour and privilege to have been asked to write a foreword. I can't wait to see the book published, and to share a couple more chapters with you before we both finally hang up our boots.

Cheers, 'H'.

Tribute

by Tony Finch

Former Warwickshire CCC committee member

It is with great pleasure and deep respect that I write this tribute for Andy, a friend I have had the privilege of knowing for over 35 years. Our friendship began with a shared love of cricket, and from there it blossomed into something much more. Together we have travelled the world, watching and enjoying the game we both love.

I have had the honour of witnessing Andy's career from the sidelines, seeing him excel not only as a gifted batsman but, more recently, as a distinguished coach. His passion for the game and his dedication to those around him have always shone brightly. Our first meeting was at one of Andy Lloyd's benefit functions, and from that day our bond grew stronger, culminating in the honour of becoming his benefit chairman and then being asked to be godfather to his son, Matthew. Even when Andy moved to South Africa, our friendship continued. We both share a deep love for the country, and together we've shared lasting memories, enjoying its wonderful wine, food and scenic trips – the perfect ingredients for many adventures and plenty of laughs.

Although Andy's career was marked by what I consider an unfortunate stroke of bad luck – being one of the few English batsmen to average over 40 in first-class cricket without being capped at Test level – his journey has been nothing short of remarkable. From playing to coaching in eight countries around the world over four decades, Andy has seen it all and achieved so much, representing England once at the Singapore Sixes, a fleeting yet memorable moment.

Andy has worked tirelessly to achieve his goals, and his resilience and passion is evident in everything he does. It is with great admiration that I wish him the very best of luck with this autobiography and with whatever his next chapter holds, whether on or off the cricket field. It is an honour and a privilege to write these words as your friend, Andy. From our debates in Finchy's bar to enjoying a South African braai at

Moler's place, we've enjoyed countless hours together. Through all the challenges we've faced, our friendship has endured, and I look forward to many more years of good times and great memories. Here's to a friendship that has stood the test of time and to whatever lies ahead.

Prologue

The elderly Afghan must have been about eighty. A caretaker-cum-floorsweeper at the hotel in Kabul which was my home in Afghanistan, he stayed in the academy accommodation of the Afghan Cricket Board, who sort of looked after him. He was a lovely man, with whom I often exchanged greetings, although he spoke no English. But he was Taliban – everybody knew it: not a fighter but just a political member. One day, when drinking some green tea with one of my assistant Afghan coaches in the hotel cafe, the old man said he had a message for me. It was delivered in the Afghan language Pashto, but I vividly recall the English translation that was later relayed back to me. "The Taliban will not attack Andy Moles because they are really happy about the effect of cricket here and what he is doing," the old man had declared. "There is a positive outlook for Afghanistan around the world through cricket. If he is in the wrong place at the wrong time that would be unfortunate. But they will not target Moles or send anyone to get him, or set up a roadblock to take him when he is in his car."

I must confess I felt a little bit easier after this reassurance, but I did become blasé about it. The more I went to Afghanistan in the six years I was employed by the Afghan Cricket Board variously as national coach, chairman of selectors and director of cricket, the more at ease I felt, which becomes dangerous. Roadblocks were a common practice if the Taliban were coming after you. My secretary, an Afghan male who looked after my admin when I was director of cricket, had been kidnapped by the Taliban before I first arrived in Afghanistan. He had driven out to his village, about three hours from Kabul by car across the mountains, and on the way back to Kabul he came round a bend and there they were, with a car parked across the road. His father was a member of parliament in Kabul. They kept him for nearly three months, roughed him up a bit, and his father had to sell off belongings to pay the ransom. The father of Afghanistan all-rounder, Mohammad Nabi, was also kidnapped when he was earning good money in the Indian Premier League. Nabi likewise had to pay a ransom to get him back. Gangs often did the kidnapping and then offered victims on to the Taliban in exchange for a fee.

Happily for me, the old man's promise was honoured. I look back now and realise I could easily have been abducted on my multiple journeys from the hotel to the national cricket ground, which was outside the so-called 'ring of steel' in Kabul. There were quite a few security incidents, which I will detail later in the book, but I suppose it is ironic that the cause of the amputation of my left leg can be traced to Afghanistan. For it was there that I contracted MRSA in an infected little toe which ultimately left the surgeon in Cape Town with no choice but to take the leg off below the knee. This happened a few weeks after my 59th birthday on the first day of lockdown in South Africa, March 27, 2020. Three months later, the Afghan Cricket Board terminated my contract in a cursory email, and I was out of work with bleak prospects for any future employment. A year or so later, however, I got a surprise call from the Bahamas Cricket Association, offering me a part-time role to coach their national team. Four years on, I'm still performing that for two or three months a year and am very grateful to them for that opportunity. It may or may not be my last coaching role, but it has been a 40-year odyssey around the world as a player and coach. From a lengthy playing career with Warwickshire and Griqualand West to my current home in Cape Town after coaching stints with Free State, Hong Kong, Kenya, Scotland, England Under-19, Northern Districts (NZ), New Zealand, University of Western Cape, South Western Districts, Wellingborough School, Afghanistan and the Bahamas. For a youngster who was on the dole in the summers from the age of 21 to 24 when my dream was to become a professional cricketer, it has been a full life I never thought would materialise.

1

Early years and Warwickshire debut

I didn't start playing the game of cricket till the age of 15. I don't quite know why I left it so late as I always wanted to play all ball sports as a youngster as they came easily to me since my hand-eye coordination was good. I was in the first teams for football, rugby, tennis and table tennis at my comprehensive school, Finham Park in Coventry. After I took the game up and made the school side, they sent me to the Coventry Schools nets practice that summer. Lo and behold, I was picked the next day in their Under-16 team. That got me hooked, although I didn't follow county cricket apart from the Roses championship match which, for some reason, was shown live on TV every year. I'd sit down at home and record every ball in a home-made scorebook. I did follow the Test matches closely, and like most young lads of that era Ian Botham was my hero. Later, he would abuse me on the field but we became quite good friends off it.

My parents were never really into cricket, but they were very influential in my footballing days as a teenager. I think Dad, from whom I inherited a deep love for Coventry City FC, aka the Sky Blues, was more excited when I played semi-pro football as a teenager than when I joined Warwickshire. By then, he had become Philippines Airlines director of purchasing and opened his own business in Singapore. He never really came back – only for a period in the early millennium. He's now 89, having lived in Perth for 15 years, and has an Australian passport and a Singaporean second wife, a lovely lady. Mum died aged 66, having moved to Spain for the weather with her second husband, who sadly died in a car crash.

I was, and remain, close to my three brothers, Mark, Paul and Simon. Mark joined the RAF and then the Met Police. He foiled a bomb plot in Dubai, where he was attached to the British Embassy, when a bomb was found in a printer after he tipped local police off. He also worked for Apple as European security adviser and was later head of anti-terrorism in Bahrain. He has now retired to Cyprus, having been awarded an MBE for services to anti-terrorism. Paul works for Land Rover, living in Solihull, and Simon, a demolition expert, has moved to Newcastle.

After my parents divorced, Mum and we four brothers moved from Styvechale, a nice area of Coventry, to a council house in Wood End, which was one of the roughest. We were belittled as the posh boys as we came from Styvechale, but I certainly wasn't the boy with the silver spoon. One day one of the local yobs picked on Mark and duffed him up a bit. I went round to his parents' house in the next block to have it out with him. I knocked but got no answer, so I gave a tap on the glass entrance door with my metal-capped boot, which I was wearing as I had come straight from my factory job. The glass shattered. I hadn't meant it to but I went home, knowing I could be in a bit of trouble. An hour later the blue lights of a police car were flashing outside our house. Mum had always said to me and my brothers never to bring the police to her door. I told the police it was a complete accident, and they were surprisingly friendly. They said that they knew about that family, and they were trouble. "But be careful – calm it down," were the last words I remember from the constable. I had got away with a warning but was in the doghouse for ten days with my mother. The feud with the other family lasted for a few months before calming down afterwards. There were plenty of other characters around you had to worry about, not just them. It was a rough area, but it toughened me up. Any aggro I experienced on a cricket field was like a Sunday picnic in comparison.

My school cricket experiences ended up being brief as I left school at 16 in the summer of 1977. I didn't think I'd done well in my exams, and I was right, passing only a couple of 'O' levels and some CSEs. My plan was to join the RAF as a PT instructor but, although the application process went well, some defence budget cuts were announced, and my draft just didn't happen. I didn't know what to do, but the job centre rang to say there was a vacancy for an apprenticeship at Brett's Stamping Works in Coventry. My father, who worked in tyres and brakes for Dunlop aircraft, told me I had better go for interview. The foreman there said I wouldn't get the job unless I told him the name of the prime minister. I had a mental blank, but then suddenly his name came to me. "Callaghan," I exclaimed. "Right you're in," he told me. "Your weekly pay cheque will be £16.66."

I can't say I enjoyed my apprenticeship, and I have to say I was awful. In my first year I went to the training centre, and in the years after I was in the factory working. I hated it. I used to work on making the dyes, ending the day really dirty. I didn't get on with the foreman and liked to wind him up; I'd clock in on the dot of 8.03 each morning, the latest you were allowed to. It drove him crazy. We were let out at noon for lunch, and had to be back by 1.03pm latest. I never returned a minute before then, as I knew it annoyed him. I was a bugger. I didn't enjoy it, but I met some good people and did just enough to keep the job. It didn't excite me, and I couldn't wait for the weekends to play sport – football in winter in the Coventry Works District first division, where I reached semi-pro level, and cricket in summer for Dunlop Sports & Community Club. But at that stage I never had an inkling of playing professional sport.

It was at Dunlop where I met Fred Gardner, who was a huge influence on my early years as a cricketer, as well as another elderly man called Alan Watkins, who loved the game. They helped get me selected for winter nets for the best youngsters, which were organised by the Coventry Works Cricket League. Fred was an important mentor to me. He used to come and pick me up from our house in Wood End in his maroon Triumph. One day he knocked on the door and I heard my mother shout, "Who the bloody hell is that at the door?" She came down and saw this immaculately-dressed gentleman. "Mrs Moles, I've come to collect your son for nets," he said. "I'm ever so sorry, sir," she replied. "I thought it was the kids next door playing around knocking at the door and running off." "Don't worry my sweetie," Fred responded. He was a lovely man, who taught me how to respect the game, how to play it hard and be confident in yourself. Ten years or so later, I met someone at Edgbaston, who told me that Fred had said to him when I was at Dunlop that I would play for Warwickshire one day.

Up until the age of 20 I played league cricket for Dunlop on Saturdays as well as for Kenilworth Wardens on Sundays which were declaration matches. As soon as I finished my apprenticeship, I moved to Birmingham in the winter of 1981/82 where there were more work opportunities as an engineer. I joined Moseley CC, whose second team captain Dick Chase worked in HR at Lucas Industries with his girlfriend Kate. They got me a job there in early 1982, working on the factory floor with machines that pump out thousands of screws. I soon got promoted from there into the standards room.

Moseley were reigning Birmingham League champions, and I had to start off in the second team in 1982. After scoring heavily in May, I got a first-team game in early June but batted at number eight. I was not happy and told the captain Mike Cheslin to promote me or put me back in the seconds, or I'd leave the club. That night at a barbecue at Chase's house, he told me to calm down and that he would have a word with Cheslin. The following week I got moved up to number five, where I got runs, and I ended the season at number three. We had a strong batting line-up that included Brian MacMillan, the future South Africa all-rounder. I learnt how to be hard and tough and not throw my wicket away.

At that time the Warwickshire second eleven also played in the Birmingham League. I got a couple of sixties or seventies against them in that season and reckoned I was as good as any of their batsmen. I must have made some sort of impression on their coach Neal Abberley as in the following year I got late call-ups up for several three-day games for Warwickshire's second eleven. I owe a debt to Gordon Lord, my good mate on the Warwickshire staff, as he told Abberley that I would definitely be available to play last-minute if needed. I was always rung on the Tuesday night when they were one short for the match starting the next day, but I didn't mind that. It just meant I had to take a 'sickie' off work from Lucas for the next three days. However, my boss there was an avid reader of the Birmingham Post and would scour the second eleven match scorecards in it. "I see there's another lad called Moles playing for Warwickshire seconds and scoring some runs," he once said to me. I've no doubt he knew it was me, as I always went down sick on a Wednesday morning, but I'm thankful to him for turning a blind eye.

Being called up last minute, however, was not good preparation, and I didn't make the impact I hoped I would. A check in the Wisden almanack shows I was second bottom of the second-team averages in

1983, with only 78 runs from eight innings with a top score of 20. But playing in these matches proved a classic case of being in the right place at the right time, for in the lunch-break of my final second eleven appearance that summer, a team-mate, David 'Diddy' Smith, asked if anyone wanted a coaching job at a school in South Africa that winter. He was giving it up to move to a better opportunity in Cape Town.

"It's a school called Gill College in the middle of nowhere in the eastern Cape near a place called Somerset East," he said. "The town has a row of shops, a hotel and two bars. That's it. Pay is 200 rand a month plus board and keep, and the return flight. "I'll go," I said. "But you've got a job," pointed out Anton Ferreira, our first-team South African 'overseas' who had dropped in to watch the seconds. "I'll give it up," I retorted. "Listen, man, you're 22, and the chances of you making it are slim," he warned, no doubt aware I hadn't scored any runs. I'd made my mind up, though. A winter coaching and playing in South Africa could only improve my game in my quest to become a professional, so for me it was not a difficult decision. Moreover, if I was going to play for Warwickshire seconds the following year, I could not have gone on taking sickies at Lucas. Dick Chase had got calls from the boss asking why I was regularly sick for three days and always on Wednesdays, Thursdays and Fridays. The boss could not keep overlooking it, so I had to leave Lucas or stay and stop taking sickies, thereby being unavailable for mid-week cricket.

That winter of 1983/84 was the first of three in succession I spent at Gill College, a hundred miles or so north of Port Elizabeth. Apart from coaching the boys, I had to play in their school team in the Karoo Men's League against other local men's teams. The cricket could get a bit tasty as some opposition fast bowlers were bullies and would tear into the young kids. I took it upon myself to protect them. There was one incident against a team called Jansenville where they had a young pace bowler who'd played for Eastern Province reserves. He roared in and bowled quick at the kids and gave them a little bit of verbal. It was a two-day match, and we had to follow-on, so I opened the batting and stayed at one end so that only I faced him. I hooked and pulled him and told him: "If you want to be a bully, be a bully to me and leave the kids alone." The head boy of Gill College walked onto the field and said, "Sir you're not conducting yourself in the manner Gill College would like you to. Please stop arguing with the opposition." It was quite funny in hindsight, and afterwards we all had a beer, but I wasn't happy at the time as these kids were only 16 or 17, playing men's cricket.

Gill College was a great experience for me – to learn how to bat for time and value my wicket. I also opened the bowling as we played with a two-piece Kookaburra ball which swung all over the place. I developed my medium-pace outswingers then, which proved very useful when I eventually made my debut for Warwickshire in the Sunday League in 1986. I've still got friends from my Gill days – local farmers mainly – that I keep up with. I loved my time there as I was playing cricket the whole time. It was all part of doing everything I could to advance my chances of playing county cricket.

I returned from South Africa to Birmingham in time for the 1984 season and signed on the dole. That at least meant I could play as much mid-week cricket as possible and prepare properly for whatever Warwickshire second eleven opportunities came along. My parents, though, weren't too happy that I was unemployed, with Dad saying, "Stop chasing the dream." I played regularly for the Midland Club Cricket Conference and spent two or three days in mid-week turning out for different guest teams, just to get as much cricket as I could. Warwickshire gave me half a dozen three-day second eleven games, but I again did not make as many runs as I would have liked, averaging 27.75 from 11 innings.

After another winter at Gill College, I came home knowing that 1985 was likely to be a make-or-break season for me. Once again, I didn't look for a job as I wanted to play cricket four or five days a week so that I was ready for any opportunity. Fearing, rightly as it turned out, that opportunities for Warwickshire would be even fewer than the year before, I wrote to every first-class county apart from Yorkshire (for whom you could then only play if born there) asking for a trial. Not one replied. I played only three second eleven games for Warwickshire that summer, none of them consecutively, but improved my average with the bat to 63.66, and topped the second team bowling averages with five wickets at 13 apiece from 23 overs bowled.

Completely out of the blue, however, came an unexpected chance that I managed to seize. The chairman of Coventry City FC, Bryan Richardson, said to me years later, when I trained with them one winter, that you will always get one big opportunity in life but often when you least expect it. Only a few people, he added, recognise it when they get it, but it is your duty to be ready when it comes. Fortunately I was in good nick when mine came along as well as being as fit as a butcher's dog. It was a testimonial game in mid-July that I got invited to play in – a joint one for Dennis Amiss and Richard Hadlee, with Warwickshire up against Nottinghamshire during the Blackpool festival week with the proceeds split between the two beneficiaries. Andy Lloyd, who'd made his England debut the year before, had had his thumb broken the day before the match, and Gordon Lord put my name forward as a potential replacement. Amiss rang me that night to see if I was available, and I could barely control my excitement at the prospect of playing in a first-team match, even if it was only a testimonial.

The festival atmosphere was embraced by Warwickshire's wicketkeeper-batsman Geoff Humpage, a real wag who liked to make out he wasn't taking the match overly seriously. We fielded first and, desperate to impress, I raced around the boundary to collect a ball and threw it in flat and hard just above the stumps. Humpage shouted across to me, "You can pack that in, young man. I'm not used to throws like that." Later, Humpage went out to bat carrying a broom, joking that sweeping was the way to play the great Pakistan leg-spinner Abdul Qadir, who was guesting for Notts. Humpage did not get runs that day, and I went out to bat at number six with Amiss still at the crease. I gave him the strike as much as possible but finished with 65 not out as we won the game. During the festivities afterwards David Brown, the Warwickshire cricket manager, came up and said to me: "Ever thought of being a pro, young man?" I replied: "Well, earlier this year I wrote to all the other first-class counties except Yorkshire asking for a trial, but didn't get a reply from any of them." Norman Gifford, the club captain, cut in and said: "Well you don't have to do that any more, son. We'll get back to you."

I heard nothing more till late August that summer when I played in the Under-25 competition final in which Warwickshire beat Kent at

Edgbaston. I opened the batting and got 19, with Asif Din topscoring with 75 in our total of 233 from 40 overs. Kent fell 45 short with McMillan picking up three for 25. During the celebrations afterwards, Abberley called me over to the dining-room where he was sitting with head coach Alan Oakman. "Now then, young man, I've been instructed to tell you that you have a six-week trial next year starting with pre-season." I was a little disappointed as all the boys had been chin-wagging and saying, "They're going to offer you a contract, Moler." Abberley added: "I suggest you make the most of it, young man." He wasn't a big fan of mine, as I was the overweight kid from Moseley who hadn't come through the system. By then I was six months short of my 25th birthday.

After a third winter at Gill College in the eastern Cape, I came back home in the middle of March in 1986, well ahead of report-back day in early April. My one problem was I had no money to buy any equipment as I'd lived off the dole for the previous three summers when I was unemployed. Lordy advised me we'd be indoors to start with, but I only had studs. I was staying in Edgbaston with my uncle and aunt, and he was living in nearby King's Heath, so we arranged to have a net outdoors by ourselves. When we met, he opened a bag and said: "Here you go, Moler. I've bought you a pair of white cricket shoes, a thigh pad and a pair of pads." I've never forgotten that he did that and probably haven't said it enough to him that he was a huge influence on the success of my trial.

Thanks in no small part to Lordy, I was as fit as a butcher's dog after the winter in South Africa. He had also been out there, playing at Graaff-Reinet, just over an hour's drive from Gill College, and we'd visit each other at weekends and train. He was a big runner and was always a bit fitter and stronger than me. On the first day back at pre-season, we had to run 18 laps around the colts ground, which was about three miles. It had to be done in under 27 mins. I did it in 21 minutes, lapping Amiss and Gifford twice with Lordy 100 yards ahead of me. I overheard Gifford muttering to Amiss, "You can see the ones that have worked hard over the winter, Dennis."

The first two to three weeks of my trial period were just nets. I had to make an impression with my passion and how hard I was prepared to work, then make runs. My first hundred in a pre-season game was against Glamorgan at Swansea. I came off and Lordy said to me, "Good players go and make another hundred." Lordy pushed me and said the right things at the right time – he was a quality human being. As it turned out, I took his job as opening batsman. He only played a couple of championship games that season, got released at the end of it and went to Worcestershire.

Lordy and I were very close. It was bitter sweet that I took his place. A mark of the man is that nearly forty years later, in the summer of 2024, he rang me after he had spent a day at the Lord's Test when he was on a train home and left a voicemail: "Moler, I know we don't speak very often these days, but you were a bloody good player. You don't know how good a player you were. I was at Lord's with a few ex-players today, and they all said you should have played for England. I'm just ringing to let you know I'm thinking of you." That was typical of Gordon. He was utterly selfless.

My six-week trial went well, and I ended it with a mountain of runs including four hundreds in a week in second eleven and club matches. Very soon after, towards the end of May, I was given my first-team debut when Ferreira pulled a hamstring in the warm-ups just before a Sunday League game against Worcestershire at Edgbaston. We batted first, and I came in at number seven, managing only 7 before I got out to Dipak Patel, the off-spinner who later played for New Zealand. I was one of four stumping victims for Steve Rhodes, which was a record for a John Player League match. Alvin Kallicharran made a hundred to take our total to 174 from our 40 overs.

I remember being barely able to contain my excitement when we were about to go out to field. When Gifford clapped his hands and said "Let's go," I jumped up right beside him whereupon he asked why I was wearing a long-sleeved sweater. I replied that it was a bit chilly out there, but he smiled: "Where you'll be fielding, you won't need it. Get it off." I was running from fine leg to fine leg across the field at the end of every over. At that stage, I was a bit of a whippet.

I came on first change and bowled tidily, claiming a maiden victim in Phil Neale whom I bowled. I might also have had Graeme Hick caught in the gulley off a thick edge but Gifford, by then 46, failed to get a hand on it. I was quite pleased with my figures of one for 25 from eight overs, but Worcestershire won the match by four wickets with four balls to spare.

In the following round of John Player League matches, I was again named at number seven in the side against Lancashire at Old Trafford. Rain reduced it to a 10-over slog, and I didn't get in as we managed 87 for three. When I came on first change, Clive Lloyd was batting and faced all six balls of my first over. I managed to restrict him to just two runs in that over by jagging it into him on a dampish wicket and cramping him up. I kept thinking the next ball to him was going to go out of the ground, but luckily enough it didn't. Although my second and last over cost 12, we managed to win the game by 11 runs. It was my first taste of victory in a first-team game and a great feeling.

It was a special weekend as the day before, on the Saturday, I had made my championship debut at Old Trafford after driving up from a 2nd XI game the night before. We got put in, with me at number seven, and slipped to 110 for four before rain washed out play for the day. On the Monday – the John Player League match being staged on the Sunday – Humpage and Din put on 183 for the fifth wicket, and when I finally walked to the crease, we only needed seven runs to reach 300 and a third batting point when I was told we would declare. Patrick Patterson, the West Indies fast bowler, was tearing in from near the sightscreen for my first ball, but I pushed a single to open my first-class account before Din hit the runs we needed for the declaration. When we fielded, I came on second change to bowl but struggled with my delivery stride as the square was elevated above the run-ups. I bowled seven overs for 30 without taking a wicket before they declared 149 behind to enable a final afternoon run chase. We set them 270 in 53 overs, and it came down to 15 off the last over with us needing two wickets. Tailenders Paul Allott and David Makinson scored ten without getting out, so it ended up as a draw.

From there we went to Bristol to play Gloucestershire in the championship. After 11 wicketless overs in the first innings, it was a relief to claim my first first-class wicket: Andy Stovold leg before. It was a high-scoring game on a typically flat Nevil Road pitch, and I didn't get to bat in our first innings. After we were set 315 in four hours on the final afternoon, we gave it a go before shutting up shop eight down for 249. I went in at number eight and made only 6 before falling to Courtney Walsh.

Gifford and Brown were excellent, managing me very well. "Just have a couple of games and get the feel. I know you want to bat higher up but you'll be fine," Brown said. I was batting at number three in the seconds where I was scoring loads of runs. That season I made 811 runs in nine matches for them at an average of 73.72 with four hundreds. So my confidence was high.

A chance to bat up the order would eventually come in mid-July when poor Andy Lloyd suffered another injury. He had his nose broken at Portsmouth, not when batting but when Kevan James slashed an edge off Gifford into his face at slip. Geoff Humpage, who had a way with words, told him he looked like a panda. The day it happened, I was playing for Moseley in a Birmingham League match against Worcester City, who had Ricardo Ellcock, the very rapid Barbadian who'd been to Malvern College on a scholarship and who would get picked for England's 1990 tour of West Indies. For some reason, there was always needle in the Moseley v Worcester fixture, which was no doubt communicated to Ellcock. When I came in at number three, Ellcock was bowling, and he roared in on a rock hard Moseley wicket and bowled me a vicious bouncer first ball which I gloved straight to short leg. I walked off thinking I hadn't even seen it.

Dave Humphries, the former Worcestershire keeper, was playing for them and said after the match, "I hear you're going down to play in the Sunday League tomorrow, Moler, but don't worry about that ball Ricardo bowled to you on that wicket, with the effort he put in. Malcolm Marshall won't bowl as quick as that. You'll be fine. Go out there, just enjoy it and play well." He'd always been a bit grumpy when we played each other previously, but that revealed there's a brotherhood among pro cricketers. Yes, we have words and fallouts with occasional finger-pointing, but after battle we're aware we're a small group of people who are fortunate to play the game for a living.

The next day at Portsmouth Marshall bowled me a bouncer to which I got inside the line and helped down to fine leg for a single. He just looked at me without saying anything, and I thought, "Oh dear, what have I done now?" I didn't get out to him, though, annoyingly falling lbw to Mark Nicholas' dibbly-dobblers for 18. We only made 152, and they knocked them off with ease, Robin Smith thumping an unbeaten fifty and Marshall a rapid cameo.

Lloyd's injury meant he was going to be out for the rest of the season. Brown came to me and said: "We want you to open – it's the same as number three, son. You don't have to wait to bat. Just go out and bat." And when I opened the batting, I took to it like a duck to water. My first opening partner was Paul Smith, when we took on Lancashire at Edgbaston. Patterson was not playing on this occasion, but his replacement Tony Murphy trapped me leg before for one in the second over of the match and we were skittled by tea for just 138. Rain washed out the second day but, thanks to a Clive Lloyd hundred, they got a big first innings lead. In our second dig, however, I made 67, sharing a stand of 51 with Amiss, who went on to score his 100th first-class hundred that afternoon and save the game.

After that maiden first-class fifty, it got even better for me with a maiden hundred in the very next match, against Somerset at Weston-super-Mare. Smith and I saw off Joel Garner in a first-wicket stand on day one of 161. I contributed 66, although during the first drinks break, our twelfth man came out with a message to stop hooking Garner as he would bowl quicker at the rest of the top order. In our second innings I applied myself diligently on a slow but true wicket and reached my hundred from 242 balls with a four down the ground off Mark Davis, the left-arm seamer. As soon as I hit it, I heard Viv Richards at mid-wicket say, "Well played, young man."

That was a compliment that meant a lot as, for me and almost every pro, he was the best batsman in the world. In Somerset's innings, after we had set them 356 to win in three hours and 20 overs, Viv blasted a hundred off only 94 balls to give us a scare, but when McMillan bowled him, the match petered out into a draw. Afterwards, Amiss said something to me that I've never forgotten: that you only learn how to bat when you've got a hundred. It was so true. Everything seems so much easier – the way you move, your balance and your shot selection. It was a jubilant drive back to Birmingham for me that night, although only a short celebration was possible as we had another championship game against Kent starting the next morning.

Eight days after my maiden hundred, I made another century – against Gloucestershire at Nuneaton, whose ground was only eight miles from where I'd grown up in Coventry. It was particularly satisfying as Gloucestershire were top of the table and had a good attack, with Walsh and the very quick David Lawrence sharing the new ball, and David Graveney and Jeremy Lloyds making up a fine spin duo.

My confidence was sky high during that month of August at the end of which I came close to scoring a third hundred, falling for 91 against Yorkshire at Edgbaston. In that match Paul Smith and I set a new world record in first-class cricket with our eighth successive half-century opening stand (four of them converted to century partnerships). For the record, the sequence was 161 & 155 (against Somerset at Weston); 77 & 57* (against Kent at Edgbaston); 60 & 102* (against Gloucestershire at Nuneaton), 63 (against Worcestershire at New Road); and 109 (against Yorkshire at Edgbaston). We actually made it ten fifty-run stands in 12 innings when putting on 50 and 93 in September against Middlesex and Sussex respectively.

Despite our success together, we didn't open again as Andy Lloyd returned from injury the next year and Paul had to drop down the order. From a personal point of view, though, a season that had started with me on a six-week trial could hardly have finished any better. I was third in the Warwickshire batting averages with 738 runs at an average of 49.20. That was a great thrill. I had learned a lot about the first-class game in my eleven championship appearances that season from the experienced players in the side – Kallicharran, Amiss, Ferreira and Lloyd – who had really looked after me. Gifford, one of England's best left-arm spinners in his time, even coached me on the outfield how to play spin as I'd basically come straight from club cricket. He was hugely helpful.

2

Griqualand West and county cap

Barely a week after the county season ended in 1986, and having signed a new two-year contract with Warwickshire, I was on a plane to South Africa to spend the winter there playing for Griqualand West in the SAB Bowl first-class competition. This was the equivalent of the modern-day second division of the County Championship, and involved Boland and the B teams of Transvaal, Natal, Western Province, Eastern Province and Northern Transvaal. Their A teams played in the Currie Cup. My Warwickshire team-mate, Gordon Parsons, had been out there the previous winter along with Laurie Potter of Leicestershire as Griqualand West's overseas professionals. When Potter decided not to go back, 'Bullhead' as Gordon was known asked me if I fancied replacing him. I jumped at the chance of another winter in South Africa.

We flew to Kimberley, the celebrated diamond mining town where Griqualand West's home ground, the De Beers Country Club, was located. Soon after our arrival, we had a three-day first-class match in early October against the South Africa Defence Force team, whom I imagined would present a similar sort of challenge to that of Oxford or Cambridge Universities in early season in England. How wrong I was. Defence, as they were known, could call on some very talented young players in South Africa, as national service was then compulsory. One of them in that match was a lean young Afrikaner speedster called Allan Donald, who was a couple of weeks short of his 20th birthday. Little did I know then that he would become one of the most feared fast bowlers of his generation and a great overseas signing for Warwickshire.

When we won the toss and took first use of a decent-looking pitch, I didn't think I needed a helmet and wore my cap. I had worn a helmet without a grill in my first season at Warwickshire as I never liked the big thick blue bar on the grill of helmets of the time as it dragged your head down. Thankfully someone soon invented a lighter one, and I got used to the grill. On that day, though, there I was batting against

Donald without a helmet. The Defence captain Roy Pienaar, who would play for Kent for the next three English summers, said to me as I took guard: "This bloke's got a bit of pace, you know – be careful." I replied, "We'll see." Donald soon bowled me a bouncer, which I top-edged over the wicketkeeper. He was decidedly quick, and within a few overs I swallowed my pride and called for my helmet. I managed to get 72 that day, but Donald picked up four for 80 as we were bowled out for a below-par 242.

Defence replied with 407, whereupon Donald proceeded to blow us away in our second innings with seven for 63. He didn't get me out but was a handful – a bit wild but he had that beautiful run-up and explosion at the crease. I top-scored with 46 but we lost by ten wickets, a heavy defeat against a decent side but one we were expected to beat. Donald did not play much more for Defence, as Free State, whom he had already represented as an 18-year old, wanted him back. That winter in South Africa, only Garth Le Roux took more first-class wickets than Donald, who finished with 47 victims at 23 apiece. I alerted Warwickshire about his potential, prompting David Brown to do a deal with Ali Bacher, South Africa's cricket supremo. They engineered his recruitment for the 1987 season, and it was me who was dispatched to collect him from Heathrow airport when he flew in from Bloemfontein.

Waiting at arrivals for Donald to come through immigration and customs, I bumped into Ian 'Gunner' Gould, the Sussex keeper and future Test umpire. "What the hell are you doing here, Moler?" he chirped. "Collecting our new overseas youngster," I shot back. "Me, too," he laughed. I can't recall who he was waiting for, but little did either of us know I was picking up a youngster who would be a superstar for Warwickshire and really embrace life in Birmingham, eventually marrying a local girl, Tina, four years after meeting her on his first night in Birmingham. I must take some responsibility for that as, wanting to help him settle in, I took him to the Old Varsity Tavern in Selly Oak, just down the road from Edgbaston. I bought him a lager shandy and was staggered when he told me it was the first alcoholic drink of his life. He admitted he had led a sheltered life in his home town Bloemfontein, where his parents were teetotallers. He made up for it, though, as he would later drink beer as fast as he bowled. He loved a few lagers at the end of a hot day in the field, and being a supreme athlete who worked hard on his fitness and flexibility he held his drink as well as anyone. Nine years after Warwickshire first signed him, they employed him as a fitness advisor when Shaun Pollock was the overseas player for the 1996 season.

That winter with Griqualand West helped develop my game enormously, particularly off the back foot on quicker South African pitches. Bowlers used to bounce me a lot, especially if I was wearing a cap, but I loved to hook and cut. My mentality was to bat as long as I could, for in that heat, which often was 40°C plus, the bowlers would really tire in the final session. There were some good bonuses we got paid. Batters got a rand per run once you'd reached 20, after which every boundary was therefore worth four rand. That was what a beer cost, so every time I hit a boundary I'd say thank you to the bowlers. That really wound them up. There were bonuses also when you reached 50, 75 and 100. Despite the heat, and unlike today when batsmen can have a drink pretty much when they want, no drinks were allowed apart from during the official drinks break. So I pretended I was susceptible to headaches and procured a doctor's special note to be allowed aspirin during play, with water of course, whenever I wanted. That also wound up the opposition as they knew what I was up to. That way I could have a drink every 30 minutes. After tea some bowlers would be on their knees as they were not accustomed to Kimberley conditions, which were basically desert-like. Once you got used to it, it was fine though, and with my regular water intake I was able to construct long innings. My tally of runs in the seven first-class matches I played that winter was 705 at an average of 64.

I was in good form, therefore, coming into the 1987 campaign for Warwickshire. Frustratingly, though, second-season syndrome probably afflicted me for the first half of the summer when, despite getting starts, I failed to convert any into fifties in the first eight championship matches. My luck changed in the first week of July when I made an unbeaten 145 against Somerset at Edgbaston. And when I scored hundreds in each of the last three matches of the season against Worcestershire and Kent at home, and Yorkshire away, I was presented with my county cap in the dressing-room at Scarborough. So too was Asif Din, with whom I shared a second wicket stand of 147 on the first day. I was the club's leading runscorer in the county championship that summer with 1,355 runs. Asif and I were respectively second and third in the batting averages behind Geoff Humpage. I didn't feel I was playing for my place any more and got a nice message from Brown who said my name was always the first on the team-sheet. "You always made me feel comfortable. We knew we had someone we could rely on," he was kind enough to say.

My confidence was further boosted by compliments from former Warwickshire stalwart Jack Bannister, who took nearly 1,200 first-class wickets for the county in the 1950s and 1960s before becoming a journalist and commentator. He wrote in Wisden: 'Moles' 151 out of 236 against Kent on a far from straightforward pitch was an impressive innings. His power off the back foot, on both sides of the wicket, is rare among English batsmen, and his all-round technique is solid enough to suggest that he has the ability to play the game at the highest level.'

The only real disappointment at the end of that 1987 season was that I had to give up bowling due to injury. I was a regular third or fourth change bowler in the Sunday League and one-day cup competitions but picked up a groin strain. It wouldn't clear up, so our physio Bernard Thomas asked for a scan that revealed osteo-arthritis. Some liquid gold was injected to line the ball-and-socket joint. I didn't bowl at all in 1988, and although I sent down a few overs in 1989 and in subsequent years it was invariably for declaration purposes to set up a contrived finish in championship cricket.

My late-season run glut was replicated when I returned for another winter in 1987/88 with Griqualand West. In six first-class matches I totalled 657 runs at an average of 65.70, and finished second only to Allan Lamb in the South African first-class averages. Lamby, who'd been in the England side that narrowly lost the World Cup final against Australia in Calcutta that November, played for Free State as he did not go on either of England's subsequent winter tours to Pakistan and New Zealand. Like him I made three centuries, including my first double hundred – against Transvaal B at Kimberley. I was at the crease for the whole of that day, a seriously hot one, and when I returned to my house that evening I found that my new South African girlfriend, Jacqui, had very sweetly put our sheets in the deep freeze. The temperature was still 36°C and we had no air-conditioning. I got home and wrapped myself in the frozen sheets. The relief from the heat as I cooled down was extraordinary. Jacqui, who was a magistrate, was a friend of the girlfriend of Don Topley, the Essex seamer who had replaced Parsons as Griqualand West's second overseas pro. She had set Jacqui and me up on a blind date, when we hit it off from the outset.

After scoring heavily in South Africa the previous winter, and spurred on by Jack Bannister's suggestions I had Test match potential, I was hoping for a bumper crop of runs in 1988. It was not to be, proving to be the only season between 1987 and 1993 when I failed to pass 1,000 championship runs. Having been capped at the end of the previous season, I moved from the uncapped dressing-room into the separate capped one. There was an alleyway between the two. David Brown told me not to sit with my mates Gladstone Small and Paul Smith, but next to Norman Gifford and other senior players. I pinned my ears back and just listened to them, learning so much. They talked about the game and the tours they had been on. Brownie managed me very very well; I have huge respect for him and Giff, who was a lovely man. It was that season that I got out lbw five or six times, falling over to the offside too easily. I always used to tap my bat on the ground in the bowler's delivery stride, but on senior players' advice, I switched to the Graham Gooch stance of standing straight with bat held high, which kept my eyes level. It helped stop me falling over.

Bannister described the pitches at Edgbaston that summer as the 'most helpful for seamers seen there since the war'. In truth they were prepared to suit our strength which was our seam attack. Gladstone Small and Tony Merrick, in particular, took full advantage to claim 75 and 64 championship wickets respectively. It was not until the ninth championship game of the season that I scored my first and only hundred of that campaign – on a slow, seaming pitch at Nuneaton against Lancashire. It was hard graft – I made 115 off 218 balls on the first day – but was pleased to do well against an international opening pair in Wasim Akram and Paul Allott. We collapsed, though, in the second innings against the medium pace of Mike Watkinson, who took six wickets, and were well beaten.

I did get some runs on the road that summer and had nearly 800 under my belt when an opening batsman's perennial fear, a broken finger, became reality for me in early August at Edgbaston against Northamptonshire when Alan Walker fractured my thumb. That night the physio gave me some cream to rub on it, unaware it was broken. He told Jacqui to massage it but the pain was through the roof. When I had an x-ray the next day, the fracture was clear.

I was out for over a month until the last game of the season in mid-September, at home to Somerset, although it was an eventful match. We were set 301 from 68 overs on the final afternoon and had a real chance after Andy Lloyd and I put on 132 for the first wicket. Needing 89 off the last 10 overs with six wickets in hand, the chase was on but we slipped behind the rate and were eight down with too many to get when the final over began. Vic Marks bowled it and dismissed Piran Holloway with the third ball. It meant that Gifford, in his 710th and final first-class appearance, had to block out the last three balls to save the match. Happily he managed to do so, despite nine men round the bat, and could retire on a suitably dignified note.

I'm often asked who was the most challenging of the great overseas fast bowlers that I faced in county cricket at that time. For me, it was a dead heat between Malcolm Marshall and Wasim Akram. As he was left-arm over, Akram was something different. Suddenly to have it coming from another angle from someone who swung it both ways at the same express pace was a real challenge. He was the best when it came to swinging the ball; he swung the new ball traditionally and reverse-swung it exceedingly well later in the game. He would also come around the wicket at you and get the ball to leave the bat. He'd pitch it up or bowl aggressively, with some very awkward bouncers. His quick shoulder action made him harder to pick up, and he'd also walk back and turn very quickly. Once he got me lbw when I wasn't ready. All of a sudden he was on you, and you were rushed and flustered. But I learnt from that, and thereafter was always ready when he walked back, so he never got me out that way again.

Moreover, there was always needle when we played Lancashire. Allan Donald used to fire into them, and Akram into us. The Lancashire boys would always noisily encourage him against our batsmen, and we would give Donald the same vocal encouragement. It was proper, full-on, hard cricket. I enjoyed those battles and was lucky enough to score hundreds against Akram. The year after my century against Lancashire at Nuneaton, we played them at Old Trafford in mid-May on a pitch that had real pace and bounce. For some reason we got invited to a drinks reception at the ground the night before the game. Allott and Graeme Fowler, who were like Pinky & Perky together and always up to something, tried to wind me up at the function. Of course, I would give as good as I got. When they started mouthing off that Akram was not just better than Donald but also faster, I sensed an opportunity to turn the tables on them. "Al, come on over," I motioned to Donald. "I've just been listening to these two who've been saying how much quicker than you Akram is." Donald replied sternly as if he'd been insulted: "We'll see about that," before turning to Fowler, who opened the batting, "and you, I'll see you tomorrow." Both he and Allott looked on with concerned expressions.

The next day we put them in on a wicket that was rock hard. Three of their boys ended up having to go to hospital, and on our side so did David Thorne after getting hit on the thumb. Keepers were taking it at head height the whole game. Fowler survived AD's opening spell but Akram, who came in at number seven, got hit straight on the chin by him and had to retire hurt. The ball got under his grill and struck him right on the point of the chin, cutting the skin and requiring stitches. To this day if you look at him closely, it's why he's got a crow's foot right there. Both Andy Hayhurst and Nick Speak had to retire hurt early on in their second innings after taking blows from AD, although both did come back later. The game got nigglier and nigglier every day. When Hayhurst went down, Humpage turned to the pavilion, which was then at mid-wicket, and shouted: "Next! Bring on the next one." Akram wasn't able to bowl in our first innings but he was in our second, getting three early wickets including mine. Phil DeFreitas also bowled well to take four, and we fell short of our target. Of my 200-plus first-class games, I remember it as vividly as any.

3

Wedding and a final winter playing in South Africa

I'd proposed to Jacqui, and our wedding day was fixed for Dec 17 1988 in the remote Eastern Cape town of Oudtshoorn, where her stepfather, a church minister, conducted the ceremony. I wasn't planning on playing another winter for Griqualand West, but when they heard I was coming to South Africa to get married, they offered me terms for another season after John Morris of Derbyshire told them the batting needed strengthening. I played their two opening first-class matches in early December and missed the third because of our wedding. We had a brief honeymoon, and I rejoined the Griquas in time for the match against Northern Transvaal B at Centurion in early January.

My unbeaten 230 there was not only my career-best but was also the highest first-class score on the ground at that time. The opposition attack was decent, including Steve Elworthy, who went on to make his South Africa Test debut. They also had a young tearaway called Donald McCosh who, two weeks later, would take eight for 39 against Eastern Province B at Port Elizabeth. Against me, though, he kept bowling short, and I pulled and hooked him. He abused me, but I kept saying "Look at the scoreboard." We built a first innings lead of nearly a hundred and, after bowling them out again, were left with 198 to win with limited time to chase it down. I soon got caught behind off McCosh, aiming a big drive. He ran past me, shouting his delight, but I put a leg out and he tripped over it before falling over in a complete heap. As I walked off and up the steps to our dressing-room, Morris was walking down with tears running down his cheeks, saying it was the funniest thing he'd seen on a cricket field. He still uses the story in after-dinner speeches. I suppose I could have been sanctioned but I got away with it, although we didn't win the game. My opening partner, Mickey Arthur, who went on to coach South Africa, made 80 but we ended up 170 for seven. Mickey was a gritty, well-organised batsman who read the game well.

It was during that winter that Morris, aka 'Animal', and I became really good friends. I got to know him very well, with each of us being blunt Midlands larrikins.

Two years before the McCosh trip, I had had a bizarre run-in with another Northern Transvaal B fast bowler at Centurion called Tertius Bosch. He was only 19 at the time and had made his first-class debut two months earlier after being discovered by Anton Ferreira in a league match, bowling 140 clicks (approximately 88mph). He'd only got the call-up on the morning of his debut when his side bowled first. At lunchtime, though, he disappeared to the bemusement of his team-mates. Not realising lunch was provided, he had gone home to have it. When he returned to the field in time for the afternoon session, he proceeded to take five for 58 as Eastern Province B were dismissed cheaply.

When Griqualand West played against Bosch, he struck me on the body in what was a hostile spell. He followed through, asked me if I was all right and said that he was sorry as he didn't want to hurt me. At first, I thought he was taking the mickey, but he was genuinely such a meek and mild guy, a lovely man. I got 41 that day, but he took another five-wicket haul. We later became friendly, and I took him a pair of Bob Willis bowling boots every year. Six years after our first encounter, Tertius made his Test debut in South Africa's first Test match after readmission to the ICC – against West Indies in Barbados in 1992. It proved to be Tertius' only Test appearance, and sadly in 2000 he died aged 33.

Officially his cause of death was a debilitating eating disease, Guillain-Barre syndrome, although when it was first diagnosed he was given an excellent chance of recovery as only 2% of its victims die from it. At the request of his sister, his body was exhumed in 2001, revealing it had been embalmed – an expensive process that can be employed to hide poisoning. A variety of poisonous substances were found but no one has ever been charged. Letters uncovered by the private investigator hired by his sister indicate that Bosch believed his wife Karen-Anne had been unfaithful. "I am hurt that the family suspects I might have had something to do with his death," she was quoted as saying in a weekly South African magazine. Their eldest son, Corbin, also a pace bowler, made his Test debut in late 2024 against Pakistan while the younger son, Eathan, is playing provincial cricket.

4

A first trophy

Having averaged 62 in my final winter playing for Griqualand West, I returned home feeling in good nick for the forthcoming 1989 season. Before it started, we played Worcestershire in a pre-season one-day friendly in preparation for the zonal stages of the Benson & Hedges Cup. When we batted, I soon hooked a Graham Dilley bouncer for four, whereupon Ian Botham shouted out from slip, "Hey Picca, we've got a happy hooker here. Let's sort him out." Gordon Lord, who'd moved to Worcestershire, wandered over to Botham and said, "Don't keep on bouncing him, the hook's the one shot he can play." "Oh, we'll find out about that," muttered Botham. Lordy then told Beefy that I was a decent guy and a good friend of his and that I loved a curry. At the end of the match, Beefy said to me: 'Come over, young man, I believe you like curries. When we play you in the championship at Edgbaston at the end of April, you can take me for a curry in Birmingham."

When the match came along, the first day was washed out, giving me an immediate opportunity to take Beefy along to a favourite curry house of mine. This was a place in Shirley called Kababish where I knew the owner, a guy called Tyre. Of course, when the staff saw Beefy come in, they were running all over the place, making a fuss of him. They wouldn't let us pay, and whenever I scored a hundred I didn't have to pay for a curry either. That was the deal: score a hundred and you get a free curry. Whenever Beefy played against us at Edgbaston, we went for a curry. We weren't mates as such but just got on well. And he'd been my idol before I turned pro. When I had my benefit year, he was my patron and helped me out tremendously. For auction purposes at my benefit dinners, he sent me an England blazer, shirt and sweater as well as an old MCC touring sweater.

That championship match with Worcestershire was a thriller, with us needing 205 on the final day, but falling one run short. We at least earned a bonus of eight extra points as the scores finished level (which

Worcestershire didn't receive), but given we needed only seven from the final over with four wickets in hand, and two off the last ball, we were disappointed not to win. I made 85 and followed it up with a hundred in our next home match against Surrey, but we contrived to lose when we should have won. Needing 212 off as many as 105 overs, we got it down to five off the final over, bowled by Mark Feltham, with last man Tim Munton and me at the wicket. I had the strike but off the second ball of the over I was bowled to give Surrey victory by four runs. It was a gut-wrenching defeat, and seldom have I felt such conflicting emotions after scoring a hundred.

Later that season, however, came the euphoria of a NatWest Trophy win in the final against Middlesex. Although my contribution on the big day was negligible – I was bowled by Gus Fraser for 10 – there was the satisfaction of an important knock in the semi-final victory over Worcestershire at Edgbaston. On a seamer-friendly pitch we had to work very hard to reach 220 for nine in our 60 overs. Wisden wrote that my 61 'held the innings together after the loss of two early wickets and the temporary retirement of Alvin Kallicharran.' Asif Din's brilliant unbeaten 94 off 138 balls deservedly won him the man-of-the-match award, but our quintet of seamers bowled superbly to dismiss Worcestershire for only 120. Without doubt, they had badly missed the injured Botham and Dilley.

The final was another low-scoring affair after we restricted Middlesex to 210 for five from their 60 overs on a slow pitch. Against miserly bowling, we slipped to 122 for five before Asif and Dermot Reeve put on a crucial 69 in 15 overs. The equation came down to 10 off the last over, bowled by Simon Hughes. Asif took a single off the first ball, whereupon Neil Smith, his confidence sky-high after a maiden first-class hundred the day before at Leeds, straight drove the only six of the match off the next delivery. It was Hughes' slower ball, but Neil had overheard some Middlesex players urging Hughes to bowl it and was waiting for one. We got over the line with two balls to spare to claim the club's first silverware for nine years. The celebrations that night were suitably long.

I made two championship hundreds that season, but my conversion rate to three figures could have been better, for I scored eight other first-class fifties and finished with 1,138 runs. The trouble is that no one remembers the fifties – my four hundreds in eight days for the seconds were what got me noticed during my six-week trial in 1986. I'd been tipped off that the England selectors had me down as a reserve opener, but I wonder what might have been if I had converted a couple or more of those fifties. I heard that the selectors were keen to pick me for the West Indies tour of 1990, but Graham Gooch, who'd taken over the captaincy from David Gower after the 4-0 Ashes drubbing in the summer of 1989, wanted Wayne Larkins instead. Apparently, there was some horse-trading. Rob Bailey, who also made the touring party, averaged a run less than me in the 1989 season but, perhaps significantly, converted four of his ten first-class fifties that year into hundreds.

5

1990 – a record year

The golden summer of 1990 is one I know many ex-players and cricket lovers will have very fond memories of. The sun shone and batting conditions were their most favourable for many years, partly due to the authorities' introduction of less pronounced seams on balls. Having been overlooked by England, though, it was very satisfying to amass my highest ever tally in championship cricket, 1,669, at an average of 49.08. Only one other Warwickshire batsman passed 1,000 runs (Dermot Reeve), so it was not as if everyone at Edgbaston was filling their boots. I also hit a first-class hundred against the touring Sri Lankans to give myself four centuries as well as ten fifties. In batting all of the first day at Swansea against Glamorgan in late July, I compiled the highest championship score of my career, 224 not out. The week before that, I had the thrill of making a hundred in my home town of Coventry against Lancashire. 'Not even the impressive Wasim Akram troubled Moles as he scored 100 not out off 276 balls,' wrote Jack Bannister in Wisden.

It was indeed a memorable July, for it had begun with the birth of my son Danny. We were playing Surrey at the Oval, and just after tea on the second day Bob Cottam, our coach, started waving at me in the field and shouting that Jacqui had gone into labour in hospital in Solihull. I left the field immediately and had to borrow one of the lads' cars as I'd left mine at the hotel that morning when Munts and I had taken the tube to the Oval. I set off at 4.30pm, the start of rush-hour in London, and had to drive through town to the M1 as the M40 didn't extend to Birmingham at that point. Then it was a dash up the M6, completely ignoring the speed limit, to the hospital in Solihull, which I reached sometime between 6.30 and 7. To my relief and joy, I made it half an hour before Danny was born. I stayed with Jacqui till about 2.30am, and then drove back to London. Munts had waited up for me, which was a top effort by him as he'd bowled more than 20 overs the day before and 33 the day before that. Surrey were seven wickets down overnight and declared half an hour or so into the final day to set us a big target. I opened the batting the next day in no fit state to tackle Waqar Younis, who yorked me for 1 and then knocked over Asif Din and Geoff Humpage in a rapid opening spell. I slept for the remainder of our innings under a table in the dressing-room until we were bowled out just before tea to lose by 168 runs. Both Keith Medlycott, who I'd got to know in the 1988/89 winter in South Africa when he played for Northern Transvaal B, and Alec Stewart brought bottles of Champagne to our dressing-room after the match to celebrate Danny's birth. It was a really nice gesture on their part.

Six years later in another championship match at the Oval, both I and my fellow opener Wasim Khan were out for ducks on the first morning. I'd never bagged a pair in my career but, when other team-mates were on one, the joker in me could not resist putting a pear in one of their shoes. I loved to tease another fellow opener Jason Ratcliffe that way. I always said that if I got a pair at Edgbaston, I would walk back through the groundsman's shed. In this match at the Oval, Ratters, who had by then left Warwickshire to join Surrey, placed a pear on the crease at each end when Wasim and I went out for the second innings. All the Surrey boys were in on it. I gently eased my pear into the outfield before taking guard, and then clipped my first ball from Martin Bicknell for four through mid-wicket. I let out a yahoo whereupon all my team-mates on the balcony dispersed and went back to what they normally did. Wasim also got off his pair, but we were both soon bowled by Warwickshire old boy, Joey Benjamin, and collapsed from 32 for no wicket to 109 all out. Another big defeat at the hands of Surrey, this time by an innings.

Pleased though I was with my tally at the end of the 1990 season, other openers also scored heavily around the country – most notably Graham Gooch who, remarkably, made as many as 12 first-class hundreds that summer. Michael Atherton, likewise, hit a rich vein of form with over 1,900 runs at an average of 71, clinching the opening spot with Gooch in the Test side. There was still a potential berth on the England A tour of Pakistan and Sri Lanka in the winter of 1990/91 to play for, but Surrey's Darren Bicknell and Glamorgan's Hugh Morris averaged 69 and 55 respectively to get the nod from the selectors.

6
My approach to batting

My biggest tenet was the theory of staying in a bubble. If I stood up tall, the bubble was bigger; if I crouched, then it was smaller. So the bubble could move, but if I didn't break it, I was in control of where the ball was going to go. I constantly used to think, 'Stay in the bubble, be compact, stay in the bubble, stay in the bubble all the time.' If I popped the bubble, that was weak – and a good chance of me getting out. Don't break it, leave the ball outside off stump and don't play away from the body especially for the first 20 minutes of an innings. Don't cut as that's playing away from the body. If I hook and pull, OK that breaks the bubble but that's a big run scoring shot for me. I'm led to believe – Lordy told me – that when Micky Stewart was talking to the England batsmen at one stage, he actually spoke about 'staying in your bubble, don't break it.' Apparently he'd heard it from somewhere and adopted it in the England dressing-room at some stage.

If I was on a bad run, it could be I was playing outside the bubble too much, or had technically got into a bad habit. I used to talk to Neal Abberley, who didn't really bring me through because I came late to the game and hadn't started in the junior programme. But he'd seen me a lot in the early years of my career, and he used to say, "Well, your grip's slightly changed or your stance has been too wide" or whatever it might have been. He'd help, and I also had videos of myself batting when I was playing well. I used to set up a split screen with me batting in a poor run on one half, and me batting well on the other to see if there were any drastic differences.

One of my first goals was to outplay my opening partner. He had to go before me. I didn't tell anybody this, of course. In my mind I was not going to be the first one out. That used to drive me mentally. Over my career I definitely succeeded in not being the first to get out. I wouldn't know the percentage but in tough circumstances – whether it be a dodgy wicket or particularly good opening bowlers – it would get me through a five or ten-over spell. "Just make sure I come out the other side of this and still be batting," I told myself. "Get off strike if necessary."

My job as opening batsman was to make sure you see the opening bowler take his sweater. If he did that after a five or six-over opening spell and went down to third man, you'd won the battle. When I was playing, some of the best opening bowlers in the world were playing in the county game, and it was their job to knock me over. If they didn't do that, it was a big feather in my cap, I used to think. Nobody likes it flying around your ears at 90 miles an hour, but some batsmen just cope with it better than others. I think I was one of those that did. I was up for the fight every time; I loved it. It was me against them. I didn't get hit much over the years. Darren Gough hit me once on the shoulder with a bouncer which I didn't quite pick up initially, although I then watched it all the way before it slammed into me. He followed through and said, "I know it hurts, Moler, rub it." I said, "Sorry, who are you?" My arm went numb, but I was not going to rub it. He was skiddy, sharp – a good man and a fine competitor.

You have to be brave opening the batting as there's no hiding place when you do. You must not be intimidated or at least you cannot show that you are. I used to think: "You've got to own your real estate: that little bit of land you're standing on at the crease. That's my land. I ain't going anywhere, this is mine. You're not going to intimidate me to get me out." It was also vital to support your partner. Yes, you had to stay there longer than him, but you must still support and encourage him. I used particularly to enjoy the battle. If bowlers came in and chirped me, I'd give as good as I got. I loved it, and they knew it. But those top West Indians never used to say a word. Courtney Walsh just looked at you; Malcolm Marshall the same. Curtly Ambrose sucked his teeth at you every now and then. The one exception was Patrick Patterson – I'd give it back to him. Wasim Akram used to say a little bit, but not a lot. Waqar Younis used to chunter, muttering things like "You fat c***".

After a game I'd think about the four openers who had played and assess if I would make the best two if they picked a composite side.

"Did I do enough in that game?" I would ask myself. I used to think about it during the match as it spurred me on. Dennis Amiss used to say to try and average one hundred runs a game if you can. I tried to do that. Amiss taught me a lot about metal preparation. He used to stand in front of a mirror and shadow bat, often naked. He'd get out of the shower, dry off and pick his bat up.

7

Improvement under Bob Woolmer

Bob Woolmer's arrival as coach at Edgbaston in early 1991 might never have taken place but for the unexpected resignation of Bob Cottam from the position in October 1990. Policy differences with the cricket committee were the reason given, although I heard it was over whether Allan Donald or Tom Moody should be the overseas player for the following season. Bob's appointment proved to be the best way forward for the club in the longer term. He brought in new ideas and infectious enthusiasm and was a big factor in our improvement.

It could easily have been a championship title in 1991 as we were unlucky to finish as runners-up, having led the table from May 28 to August 26 and won the same number of matches, 11, as champions Essex. Our pace attack was the key, with AD bowling magnificently to claim 83 wickets and totally vindicate the decision to retain him as our overseas. Tim Munton, with 71 victims, also bowled superbly, with Dermot Reeve and Gladstone Small chipping in with 45 each. I finished with 1,246 runs at an average of 33, but it was not enough to gain a berth on the England A tour to the Caribbean the following winter. My mate Don Topley's revelation that Gooch had referred to me as "a journeyman" in the Essex dressing-room made me doubtful about my chances of international recognition. But 1991 marked the start of a marked upturn in the fortunes of Warwickshire under Woolmer that would culminate in our treble-winning year of 1994.

It was Bob who identified that we were not scoring quickly enough against spin in one-day cricket – around 4.5 runs per over. We were too often falling short of target totals by about 30 runs. The solution? Become masters of the reverse sweep, which was nothing like as common a shot as it is now. Every batsman was therefore instructed to practise it over the winter of 1991/92 to have it grooved for the new season. The next year we all played the reverse sweep and, largely as a result, our one-day run-rate climbed by more than a run to between

5.5 and 6. The reverse sweep was not a shot I'd utilised previously, but I had to be brave enough to commit to playing it in the middle. The first time I did was against Adrian Pierson of Leicestershire who had been on the Warwickshire staff before moving to Grace Road. "You don't play that shot," he shouted as I ran past him after playing it. "I do now," I retorted. And I was grinning as it went for four. "So you've joined them and everyone's playing it," he muttered, clearly surprised.

When we played Lancashire Mike Atherton was at backward point and was moved around in the ring, but I still played it. "Why are you playing that shot?" he asked. "Because it's an easy single every time," I replied. "Every time you're there, it'll go over there instead." We'd practised it that much, but opposition sides couldn't understand why we played it so often. But it was six runs an over – three runs for each batsman. We became so familiar with it that it was like playing a forward defensive. That was the reason why, batting-wise, we started to turn round our one-day form. We specifically worked on playing spin better to increase our run-rate because the coaches had identified that area as why we weren't being successful. People were bowling 25-30 overs of spin on some occasions, and we'd be 35-40 runs short just on singles.

Seamers, for their part, got cute with their slower balls and yorkers, which they brushed up on, and the fielding got better and better. When Donald bowled his slower ball, it never carried if they nicked it. So Woolmer got AD to give a signal to wicketkeeper Keith Piper or to mid-on, who would kick the ground. Piper would do a leg extension, so that third man and long leg went squarer rather than in further. So everyone was watching Pipes. The slips and Pipes would actually walk in. No one noticed at first, but Nicholas was the first one when we played Hampshire. So he waved his bat at the non-striker's end to alert the batsman on strike. But as he was always looking at Nicholas, he was often put off. We were adapting, and the opposition tried to adapt against us. AD got many out that way.

The other thing about Bob was he was the first coach to introduce video analysis. In one British winter in Cape Town where he lived, he took me out somewhere in Durbanville to an IT company who he was working with. The idea was for them to track each ball to mark where it pitched – back-of-a-length, outside stump, what shot was played etc – and you store that as data. And it was all in a dropbox, so at the end of the day you could click on, say, forward defensives and all the forward defensives that day would come up on the video. Bob was the first one who invented all that stuff; now it's all over the world and everybody does it. Bob thought ahead of his time and was a brilliant thinker of the game.

Bob was definitely the best coach I played under. He challenged you, and he liked it if you ran your own ideas past him. On pre-season tours, against select teams, I used to ask Bob whether I could play for the opposition as I wanted to face our bowlers rather than theirs because they weren't anywhere near as good. I said: "I need to be tested and put through the mill now before the start of the season. I'd rather face ours as I'll get the maximum preparation out of it." Bob happily agreed. If we had, say, four games in Cape Town on a pre-season tour, I'd play in two of them on the opposition side. Our attack was so good that it used to push me to the limit. AD would run in and bowl at 90%, which was quicker than most bowlers I would face. Nets were something I took very seriously against our bowlers, as preparation was the all-important thing for me. Gladstone Small said at a recent dinner that the bowlers enjoyed bowling at me as I would treat every ball on its merits. I got a lot out of facing those guys, and he said he got a lot out of bowling at me.

Bob used to talk about a successful cricket team as being like a table with four legs; if one is weak, the table rocks. The four prerequisites were, first, a good set of players with good practice facilities; secondly, good captain and coach; thirdly, good selection; and lastly, good administrators. If you've got all four of those, and they're all stable and trusting, the table is rock solid. If one is out, it rocks. He used to talk about that often to me: a bit when I was a player and a lot when I was a coach. Everywhere I've been successful, that has been borne out. He used to challenge you with three aspects of the game: technical, mental and physical. If you were on top of the first two, he would urge you to work on your physical side. If you were on top of physical and technical, then to work on your mental application. He'd look at simple things like "What have you done today to improve the team, or what have you done today to improve yourself?" Just little things, like "Improve yourself by 1% every day."

When you come to practice, and this is something I use all the time, there's two types of cricketer. One is a pro, and the other is the true professional. The former turns up, plays his cricket and takes his pay at the end of the month but takes short cuts and has a short career; the true professional works at his game, works to improve team environment, contributes to the team's success and also to his team-mates' betterment as well. I've found that to be very true. Northern Districts New Zealand was the best team and dressing-room environment that I had as a coach. James Marshall, the captain, was excellent. If we'd had a bad day, he'd often come off and say to me to take it out on him first as they would then know I wasn't just taking it out on them. He and I had a great working relationship.

Woolmer was a great character. He'd turn up at a Test ground – and Paul Smith used to take the mickey out of him when he did this – and stand looking out over the playing area and mutter under his breath, "Best on here ... 150 and three for 30." Once when we went to Old Trafford, Smithy had researched what Bob's best performances were there and interrupted him before he could declare them. "I know, it's 133 and two for 25. I've been listening to you for the last month, and every ground we go to there's you reciting your best figures on each, whether it's Test or county cricket." Bob looked at him and said, "Well it's true," but Smithy had caught him out. It just underlined Bob's obsession with stats and figures.

Although we slipped to sixth in the championship in 1992, our one-day form improved under Bob. Then, in 1993, after two semi-final defeats in the previous two years, came our extraordinary last-over triumph in the NatWest Trophy final that would give us so much belief going into 1994. Sussex's total of 321 for six from their 60 overs was the highest ever made in a Lord's final, and when I was soon out, flashing at Tony Pigott, and Ratcliffe was bowled by Franklyn Stephenson, we were 18 for two and in trouble. Paul Smith, though, made a valuable 60 and, just as they had done in the 1989 final, Asif Din and Dermot Reeve shared another match-winning stand, 142 in 23 overs. Asif's 104 from 106 balls was the innings of a lifetime, but when he got out, we still needed 16 off the last seven balls.

Crucially, Dermot scampered a single to take the strike for the final over, bowled by Stephenson. He did well to burgle 13 off the first five balls, giving Roger Twose the task of two off the final ball, the first he had faced. David Smith, who had made a fine hundred for them, now stood two yards from Twosey at silly point and jumped goalkeeper-like to try to block any attacking stroke, but by sheer good luck, Twosey thick-edged his drive just over backward point's head. He hared back for the second run to clinch victory and avenge our defeat to Sussex in the 1964 final. Dermot finished with 81. Our celebrations were wild, as in those days successful chases of that magnitude were very rare. Gladstone Small and I were the last two to leave the dressing-room late that evening – a good half-hour after the last of the lads who had walked over the road to our hotel opposite Lord's. We literally went round hoovering up whatever champagne or beer had been left, whether from half-finished bottles or cans. Back at the hotel we and scores of supporters partied long into the night.

As Jacqui had had our second son, Matthew, that summer of 1993 – thankfully between fixtures in May – it was always going to be a winter at home for me in 1993/94. I got some work with West Midlands Bus Travel, helping in their hospitality department. It was a dream job, entertaining guests in the company's box at Villa Park, which seated 30 guests. All I had to do was chat them up and bring up a couple of other Warwickshire players to talk to them during Aston Villa home matches. Limousines would pick me up at 11am, then collect guests before bringing them to head office at 1pm. Champagne and other wines were served over a gourmet lunch there. A luxury bus would then take us all to Villa Park, and transport everyone home at 7pm. The downside was I put on one hell of a lot of weight, so I went on the Cambridge diet in January, so that I could train properly in February and March ahead of the new season.

8

1994 – the treble-winning year

We had a pre-season tour to Zimbabwe in early April and were playing a one-day game against a Matabeleland XI in Bulawayo. I was batting on a flat track with Paul Smith against the Zimbabwe medium-pacer Guy Whittall. In between overs I told Paul, "This guy is right up your street. Just hit straight through him. It's a good wicket and he can't bowl at you." Off the very next delivery, Smithy smashed the ball back down the wicket, but it was straight at me and I couldn't get out the way. The ball hit me on my arm guard, but my arm was broken by the force of the blow. It was only a hairline fracture but a freak injury that was enough to keep me out for three to four weeks.

While we were in Zimbabwe, we thought the Indian all-rounder Manoj Prabakhar was to be our overseas player for the season. He had been Reeve's selection as he wanted to focus on one-day cricket, which was his forte and what turned him on. His preference was an all-rounder in Prabakhar, but when it emerged Prabakhar had an ankle issue and might not last the season, Dennis Amiss and the committee got onto MJK Smith, who was England's tour manager in the Caribbean, to sound Brian Lara out. Lara was one of the hottest properties in cricket, even before his 375 in the fifth Test, but Reeve still wanted Prabakhar rather than Brian. He was over-ruled by the committee, who paid Prabakhar off and then signed Lara. It was a stroke of luck that no one else had recruited him, but Reeve was not happy he had not got his preferred overseas. That was the start of why those two didn't get on.

Only eleven days after his world record score in Antigua, Lara made his Warwickshire debut against Glamorgan at Edgbaston and hit a brilliant 147 from 160 balls. Twosey dug in with an unbeaten 277 in just over ten hours as we amassed the county's joint highest total, 657, to set up an innings win. In our next match, at home to Leicestershire, Lara scored hundreds in both innings, and when we then went down to Taunton to face Somerset he made it four hundreds in as many innings. In our next encounter, against Middlesex at Lord's, he scored 140 in the second innings.

I have to admit it was terribly frustrating to see Lara score these runs and not to take part. I attended all the match days at Edgbaston where I was allowed by our physio to ride a static bike slowly for an hour, after which I'd watch the game for a while, have a shower and go home. The club suggested I go on holiday to Spain or somewhere, but I wanted to watch the boys and support them. But just as the arm had healed by late April, I started getting pains in my back. One of the club doctors, who was also on the committee, asked me about it. I told him it was bad at night but eased off during the day. He said straightaway that it could well be appendicitis. Off I went to hospital, where his diagnosis was confirmed, and after having an operation I was out for another four weeks. I had to wait for the wound to heal, with no running, bending or lifting allowed in that time. Gratifyingly Bob and Dermot called me in during my recuperation period and said: "Just get yourself some runs in the second team, and you'll be straight back in the first team. You are our number one opener."

When I was eventually passed fit to play, I went to Northampton to play in a second-team game where David Capel, the England all-rounder, was playing for them. I saw him off and got a big hundred and, as I walked off the ground, I said to Neal Abberley: "Please give Bob a call, and tell him I'm ready. I can play next week." He responded: "They ain't worried about you, son. Lara's just got 501 against Durham." I knew he'd been 111 not out overnight but couldn't believe he'd scored another 390 runs in that one day himself. It was a new world record for a first-class score, as well as being the most anyone had ever scored in a day, and I'd missed seeing it. While delighted for Brian, I was gutted not to have witnessed it, and my disappointment was compounded when they kept the same eleven the following week against Kent despite management's assurances I would be straight back in the side. I stayed in the seconds, and got another hundred, but was brought back into the first team the week after, for Northamptonshire away.

This was an extraordinary match where so much happened, including a bust-up between Lara and Reeve. As it was my first match of the season, I had not been privy to the tension that had existed between them, but I had heard rumours that Reeve had even talked of dropping Lara because of his poor time-keeping. Dermot argued that we could not have one rule for Lara and another for everyone else. When we batted first, Brian scored 197 off as many balls to equal Don Bradman's 1938/39 record of eight first-class hundreds in 11 innings. The one bowler he failed to get after was Curtly Ambrose, scoring just 12 runs off the 45 balls he faced from him. Ambrose also split his helmet when he was on 170. No one else even reached 40 that day, which we ended 448 for nine.

That evening Lara, Munton, Twose and I had a few pints in the pub by the ground. When we left, Brian decided we'd go to the McDonalds on the way back to the hotel. The bill came in and was about £8. He gave the girl serving us a £20 note, and said to keep the change. We nearly fell over as a £12 tip was a lot in those days. "What are you doing?" we asked Brian. "Well, we've had a good day, haven't we?" he replied. "Why can't she have a good day?" He just peeled off £20 from a wad of notes he had with him.

When we were in the field the next morning, Dermot and Brian had an ill-tempered exchange of words about captaincy. After the fracas, Brian walked off, ostensibly on the grounds that he was suffering a headache because of the blow on the head from Ambrose. He may well have been, but the reality was that he was miffed with Dermot's captaincy. Dermot, for his part, felt Brian was undermining him. There might have been some jealousy on his part that the media were only really interested in talking to Brian rather than him. Other team-mates believe it ate away at him. Brian didn't field again in the match, missing twelve hours in the field over both innings.

Before play on the third day, and before Brian had got to the ground, there was a discussion in the dressing-room what to do about the situation. Twosey, who was a money man, said he'd done some maths. "Without Brian Lara we are potentially likely to get approximately a £4,000 bonus at the end of the year, but with him £40,000." That caused a stir naturally enough, for whatever money we won the club matched it and the sponsors did too. "What I suggest," Twosey continued, "is we let him do what he wants to do but we cannot afford to let ourselves fall into his trap. We must be at the ground by 9am and start warmups at 9.30. Our prep doesn't change, but we do it with ten men. What suits him is because he's from the West Indies; let him prepare his way. We prepare our way, he prepares his way, even if it means turning up at 10am." That's what carried it with the boys, and Dermot had to swallow it. They never got on – they didn't respect each other. They were both driven by egos – and there was only one winner in that respect, unfortunately for Dermot.

Lara could not bat until number seven in our second innings when we needed to score 228 in 38 overs. He made only 2 but we got home with three balls and four wickets to spare, thanks to Dominic Ostler's 87 off 80 balls. The row between Brian and Dermot almost certainly led to a compromise as far as the captaincy was concerned, for Dermot, having played the first seven championship matches, only appeared in one more that season, in early August. He had a niggling hip injury and would have found it hard to play all formats, so Tim Munton took over as captain of the four-day team. Dermot still captained the one-day side and did so brilliantly, missing only one match all season. Lara liked playing under Tim, though. He had little respect for Dermot but did for Tim, who did all the right things. Munts led from the front with the ball, didn't shirk hard work and was a good communicator. Dermot liked to do things his way – a little bit quirky, a bit different – which I don't think went down well with the West Indian psyche. So they were never going to get on.

Of the nine championship games Munts captained, we won eight. Perhaps our best victory of the season – and certainly the one I remember most fondly as Munts, who is my best mate, and I made key contributions – was at Guildford in mid-July. Going into the game, Surrey were top of the table, and our chances did not look too bright when we slumped to 52 for five on the first morning. Three days later, however, we had won by the massive margin of 256 runs to make a real statement. After we had recovered to score 246 in our first innings, Surrey cruised to 107 for one before collapsing to 143 all out. Roger Twose, who only bowled because Paul Smith was unable to after being struck on the right hand, while batting, took a carer-best six for 28. I then got my head down to make an unbeaten 203 in nine hours and 22 minutes, which was believed to be the slowest double-century in championship history. We set them a notional 503 and bowled them out with over two sessions to spare, with Munts claiming five wickets to go with his four in the first innings.

Munts continued his great from with ten wickets in our next match against Essex at Edgbaston to set up a 203-run win. He then took another nine wickets the following week against Derbyshire at Chesterfield to give him 42 wickets in his last five matches. No less remarkable was Keith Piper's eleven dismissals in the match, a club record. He also became the first keeper to claim seven victims in an innings in consecutive matches, having also performed the feat against Essex. Victory, our sixth in succession, took us to the top of the table for the first time in the season, and we remained there till we clinched the title. The match was notable for yet another hundred by Lara – before lunch on the first day – when he murdered their bowling on a green pitch. Sixteen wickets fell that day but Lara was on another level to the rest of us, although he was dropped at slip on 25 off Devon Malcolm.

In our second innings, Devon bowled at the speed of light with the new ball and in great areas. For about three or four overs he gave Brian a real working over – he was ducking, weaving and hopping around at the crease. As we walked off for tea, he said: "Moler, that was his fun. After tea, it'll be my turn." When we came back on, his bat was like a wand, smashing the ball here, there and everywhere as he raced to another fifty. Derbyshire had a guy at backward point who was about 45 yards back because of the pace Brian was hitting the ball, which was flying everywhere. It was magnificent to be at the other end and watch. In the end, Dev just met his match, as a lot of people did that year against Brian. He got 2,066 championship runs that summer off only 2,262 balls. It gave us the time to bowl sides out twice.

I didn't play in the match against Middlesex at Lord's, but the boys told me about the time Brian came down the pitch to John Emburey but was beaten in the flight. Brian just let go of the bat with his bottom hand and followed through with the top hand. The ball landed on the south turret of the pavilion, which is unbelievable. Everybody was in awe of Brian; he was just phenomenal. Good players own that piece of crease they bat on, but he owned the bloody ground. He just sauntered onto the field. He didn't believe spinners could bowl; he invariably got the better of Shane Warne, who dismissed him only seven times in 20 Tests at an average of 55 runs conceded. "Step and fetch" was Brian's view of spinners.

Batting with Lara was not always straightforward. The hardest part was he'd score at such a rate that it drew you into trying to do the same. But it often became too risky to attempt, and you'd just get out. When I had a drink with the former England opener, Tim Curtis, with whom I got on well, during a game against Worcestershire later in the season, he asked me what it was like to bat with Lara. "You just can't get your rhythm," I replied. He said it was exactly the same with Graeme Hick, and that it was much better to bat at your tempo and let the more gifted player do what they do. We agreed that you just have to keep telling yourself to stay there and do what you do well. He added: "Don't get dragged into what's happening the other end and into thinking it's easy because it isn't. Stay in your lane." It was good advice.

Brian's performances nevertheless instilled confidence and belief in the team. You just did not believe he would not score any runs. And when he didn't, somebody else did. Twose and Ostler both passed 1,000 runs for the summer, and I averaged 50 from my eleven games. Brian kept himself to himself a little bit at times, and if he was a bit prickly to people outside the dressing-room he wasn't inside it, except towards Dermot. But the rest of us got on all right with him. Brian wasn't too keen to sign anything for Dermot to make money in his benefit year. Dermot would try and slip some things of his own in with the stuff the club left out for players to sign but, after a while, Brian caught on and wouldn't sign any odd stuff as knew it was for Dermot.

On the first day Brian turned up at Edgbaston in April, there was a set of new Wilson golf clubs sent to him by the manufacturers along with 375 balls to commemorate his score against England. He'd never played golf before but caught the golf bug after having some lessons and couldn't leave it alone. That's why some days he was late. He used to go down to the Belfry and do nine holes before play, getting up early and teeing off at 7am. He'd then come straight to the ground from the golf course. The Belfry were only too pleased to have the world record-holder playing on their course, so he didn't have to pay any green fees. He moved into a flat on the Dudley Road, which was a palace apparently, all paid for by the club. In the living-room was a big crystal chandelier. One day he decided to have a practice swing with his golf clubs but he connected with the chandelier and dragged the whole thing off the ceiling.

Brian used to practise hard. He came to us that year as Allan Donald was on tour with South Africa that summer, but AD lived in Brum with his wife and, before the tour started, came to bowl at us in the nets. I came out of them one day, and Brian walked down with three spring-loaded stumps on a base and placed it at right angles to the popping-crease on a line of off stump. That was the only stump the bowler could see. He had an entire net to check if his backswing was straight and not crooked. It sounds easy to do, but I've tried and you just can't bring the bat down without hitting those three stumps. Somewhere the bat hits the stumps going down or coming up. Brian refined just his hitting areas. He practised hard – not long but smart. He also worked on his slip catching, but I never saw him bowl in the nets. He would stand around and watch other people bat and, if he had something to say, he'd pass on a little message here and there. It was mainly to the effect that "If you get in today, keep going and don't throw it away." He took an interest in everyone else's mental well-being.

Midway through that 1994 season, I remember Brian sitting in the stands after some net practice and calling Twosey, Ostler and me over. "Look here, you three guys, I want you to think about what motivates you," he said. "Money motivates me – I've got one or two trust funds in London that pay me £10 a run. Whenever I feel a bit low in the middle, I say to myself 'No, no, I'm not gonna throw this away. I'm gonna make some money.' That brings me back into the zone. You guys gotta think about something – your wife, your girlfriend, your kids or whatever it is – but you've gotta find something that will make you concentrate when the going gets tough." Mine was my two kids; whenever I went out to bat, I imagined they were sitting on the edge of the ground watching me play and I couldn't let them down. So whenever I felt I was in a difficult patch, or loose in my innings, I just thought my kids are here, I can't let them down. It brought me back into total focus. That's what worked for me, and Brian started that idea for me.

We came so close to a quadruple that season, which I think would have been achieved had we not lost the toss for the NatWest Trophy final. It was definitely a-win-toss-win-game as there was so much damp around and it was a dark, foggy, horrible day on the Saturday when there was no play after 12.25pm, with us 88 for three after 29 overs. We had to restart our innings on another damp moist morning on the Sunday, and despite Lara's 81, we managed only 223 from our 60 overs. In much easier batting conditions, Worcestershire knocked off their target with eight wickets and more than ten overs to spare.

I couldn't force my way back into the side for the Benson & Hedges Cup final as I hadn't played any of the earlier rounds due to unavailability, and we quite understandably stuck with the side that got us to Lord's. I was there, of course, in the dressing-room to lend support, and for some reason we all had to go out before the match started to sing the national anthem. I didn't feel it was right I went out as a non-performer, and moreover I was dressed in a club blazer, but Gladstone dragged me down and said, "You're coming with us, you're part of this." That's why we were successful; we each looked after each other. For some reason we all knew when someone was feeling left out. There was great camaraderie.

I'd managed to get myself back into the side by the quarter-final of the NatWest Trophy. The semi was against Kent, which we won on a bowl-out after rain prevented any play. For some reason Kent thought we'd done something with the covering, or Brumbrella, as it was nicknamed. They wanted to play the game in Kent, but we said we'd play at a club ground in Birmingham. We didn't seem to get on. They were never challengers in the championship but were a good one-day side. We knew them as 'F***ing Kent' – we were convinced there was a bit of jealousy and that they thought they were better than us, but we kept pipping them. Dermot found a way for us to win as captain. That was the difference between captains. His big thing was never be afraid to try something. His attitude was that 'Whatever happens we will find a way.' His cricket brain was exceptional; his mantra was always to be positive in the dressing-room. He didn't have much of an effect on me as I backed my ability, but it did on others. For example, there was no criticism if you were out to a reverse sweep, and no blame if you got out trying something. He enforced that positivity in the dressing-room and in team meetings. If you practised it and it failed, no problem – but if you did it without practice, then it was an issue. Bob Woolmer was fully in agreement with him on that score.

Dermot didn't like it when players got out and blamed the wicket as that put doubt in the minds of batters that had still to go in. So you weren't allowed in a dressing-room environment to talk negatively about the game. It was absolutely key, in his mind, to keep positive mindsets in match situations. If you had something negative to say, it was better you didn't speak. If you had something positive, then you could throw it into the arena by all means. People could see if the wicket was doing a bit and batters were struggling. But they didn't need to be told about it.

In the summer of 2024, we had a big 30th anniversary celebration dinner in Birmingham for 500 people that was an emotional reunion for us players. A few couldn't make it but Brian did – eventually – and was excellent. The poor guy had a bit of a nightmare getting from London to Birmingham after being directed to the wrong train by a well-wisher at Euston. Munts had organised first-class train travel for him from London, arriving at New Street station at 5pm for the 7.30pm dinner. So there was plenty of time for any contingencies. Munts got a call just after 5pm from Brian saying he'd missed his train but "it's not what you think, not what you think." Apparently when he got to the station, an Indian cricket fan recognised him and said he knew the right platform for his train but put him on the one to Manchester. So poor Brian and his girlfriend went all the way to Manchester, then had to catch another train back to Birmingham. So he rocked in to the dinner at about 8.15pm. We were all going, "Oh typical Brian," but he came in and pointed to us at our table, pleading: "Boys, it's not what you think. It wasn't me this time. I turned up early and got put on the wrong train. I know what I was like, but I'm not like that any more. I apologise for all those times I was late, but I'm not like it any more." His girlfriend told us that he had kept saying earlier that day: "The one thing I can't do is let my boys down tonight. I used to do it all the time but not tonight."

Brian went round every single table – and there were fifty – and he apologised for being late. It was magnificent, and he showed himself to be a really nice guy. Everybody loved him; they didn't care he turned up late. He got up and was supposed to speak for 15 minutes but he did half an hour. He took questions and said how much he'd enjoyed 1994 and how he looks back on it with such fondness. He was wonderful, and it was a great night. To see the others was special for me too as, living in Cape Town, I don't get to see them very often. Nick Knight was compère, and it was very sweet of him to announce off his own bat that "We've talked about a lot of players here tonight, but there's a fellow sitting down here, my old opening bat partner, Andy Moles, who was a better player than me when they picked me for England. I'm not just saying that because he's here. I'm telling you, Moler, you should have played that Test match when I made my debut for England against West Indies at Old Trafford in 1995." I was quite moved by what he said, but what I've never revealed to him was that Micky Stewart told me I was going be picked ahead of him for that Manchester Test but wasn't because I had snapped my Achilles.

It was a great all-round evening. We've just got to wait another decade, and we'll do it all over again in 2034. Dermot didn't make it as he said his wife wasn't very well; nor Jason Ratcliffe, Trevor Penney and Dougie Brown, while Gladstone Small was abroad with one of his sports tours. Their absence took the edge off it a little bit, but there were still a lot of players present. More than three decades on, I remember the enjoyment in the team that golden summer for each other's success. The warmth you got back from the team was special. When you scored a hundred or took five wickets, there was genuine love for that person. And after every game, Twosey would say, "It's gone up another 1,500 pounds, the team kitty, boys. Keep going." He kept the tally, and it totted up.

I knew what my role was in the side: to protect the middle order valuables from the new ball. We all had talks regularly about it with Woolmer and the rest of the team. As for Lara, we all said to let him get on with what he does. We all recognised his was absolutely something special. We were pretty good with what we did as a group, that's why we won the championship. Ray Illingworth, the then England coach, nevertheless said he thought we were an average side, which probably explains why only Keith Piper got an England representative call-up that winter – on the Lions tour. Mark Nicholas, the Hampshire captain, countered that if Warwickshire were average, it dd not say much for the rest of the counties. I felt for Twosey, who had delayed making himself available for New Zealand until the end of 1994 when he realised his England ambitions would not be realised.

Tribute

by Brian Lara

Warwickshire & West Indies cricketer

It takes many hands to make something magical, and that's what we had in '94, my first season with the Bears. What a year. What memories. The kind of stuff that never leaves you. What we shared that summer left its mark on all of us, pulling us together for all time.

And so many characters. Just look around that dressing room. What to say of Moler? That he was funny, a great team man, that he played the game with a smile, and that no one was more generous, either at the crease or at the bar. And he could bat, man. No doubt he could play. What he did for us at the top of the order helped give the rest of us the space to do our thing behind him. A top county opener who loved it against the quicks. And then a successful coach all around the world, sharing his passion for the game and no doubt his wit and humour too.

It's great that he's written this book. I wish him every success.

9

1995 – league and cup double

The trophies kept coming in 1995 when we retained our championship title and won the NatWest Trophy Final. It could have been another treble as we were runners-up in the Sunday League, narrowly missing out on run-rate to Kent, the champions, whom we thrashed in the final game. Had our penultimate game not been rained off when victory looked likely with Derbyshire struggling on 81 for five off 25 overs, we would almost certainly have finished ahead of Kent. But six trophies between September 1993 and September 1995 confirmed us as the premier county in the country.

Sadly for me, I snapped an Achilles at the end of June and did not play again that season. A few months later in the winter, while doing a Level 3 coaching module at Edgbaston, Micky Stewart, who was the ECB's director of coaching, took me aside and said, "Moler, you deserve to know that England would have picked you for the fourth Test against West Indies at Old Trafford had you not done your Achilles. Instead, we gave Nick Knight his debut." I had mixed emotions on hearing this as I was left to wonder what might have been but I'm grateful to know that the selectors thought I was good enough. I was 34 and knew deep down that this was my last opportunity.

The irony was that I sustained the injury while batting with Knighty in a NatWest Trophy first round tie against Somerset at Edgbaston. He called me for a single to mid-wicket, then said no before saying yes again. Setting off then stopping, then setting off again did for my Achilles. I felt a sharp pain but batted on for a couple overs in discomfort before Peter Willey gave me out, leg before to Mushtaq Ahmed for 90 on the stroke of lunch. As we walked off, I asked Willey how close to pitching outside leg stump the ball had been, but he just replied, "I've done you a favour giving you, Moler. You need to get that leg checked out." He was right. I went straight to hospital where the x-ray confirmed the Achilles had been ruptured.

What was so frustrating was that I had been in such good form from the first day of the season when I made 67 in the Champion County v England A match at Edgbaston. In the nine first-class matches I played that summer before being ruled out for the rest of it, I made 710 runs at an average of 44. My 131 against Somerset at Edgbaston was particularly pleasing as we had been set 301 in 80 overs to win, and I steered us to an improbable victory, only getting out when the scores were level. It was one of 14 wins out of 17 championship matches played that summer, the highest percentage (82.35%) in county championship history, beating Surrey's 82.14% in 1955. Ours could have been higher but for a narrow 7-run loss to third-placed Northamptonshire. Allan Donald took ten wickets in that match, but so did Anil Kumble, who spun them to victory on the final day with seven victims when we were set 275. Both captains – Dermot Reeve and Allan Lamb – described it as the best championship game they had ever played in.

Dermot did a brilliant job as skipper that summer in both one-day and four-day cricket. Having missed half of the 1994 championship campaign, he played 15 four-day matches in 1995 and inspired so much self-belief in the team. Tim Munton missed the first five games due to a back operation and, with Dermot also out briefly, I had the thrill of captaining Warwickshire for the first time – against Lancashire at Old Trafford in mid-May. We lost the game, badly missing the bowling of Donald, Munton and Reeve. AD had a fabulous summer, finishing with 88 wickets at just 15 apiece. Dermot handled him cleverly. In the last match I played before my Achilles went, against Yorkshire, AD performed his customary demolition job on the Tykes, skittling them for 95 with five for 21 on a flat first-day wicket. In the second innings he broke Martyn Moxon's thumb after he and Michael Vaughan had put on a century opening stand. Having reached 179 for two, Yorkshire suffered a sensational collapse to 185 all out, giving us our sixth successive victory against them. AD had a complete mental hold over them. That win was one of four by an innings that summer to go with five by ten wickets and one by nine wickets. We steam-rollered sides.

The annoying thing was I picked up a bit of a calf strain, which can lead to Achilles problems, while I had trained at Coventry FC in the winter of 1994/95. I did three days a week with my boyhood club on Tuesdays, Wednesdays and Thursdays. Phil Neal and Ron Atkinson were the managers. I loved it as I was given a squad number and was treated like a pro. I used to wear whatever the players got and changed in the first-team dressing-room, thanks to my mate Steve Ogrizovic, the goalkeeper who was a useful seamer for Coventry & North Warwick in the Birmingham League. Steve loved his cricket and would play under a pseudonym as there were times he couldn't let Coventry FC see he was playing cricket in case he got injured. I trained with the second team but joined in first-team drills whenever needed.

10

Tales from the county circuit

Pop guns & cannons

We were playing at Taunton one year, and I was opening the batting with Roger Twose. Taking the new ball for us was Allan Donald and Gladstone Small, while Somerset had Neil Mallender and Adrian Jones. I really liked both those opponents; they were great characters and good human beings, who I really enjoyed playing against and seeing in the bar afterwards. I loved playing against Jones as he bowled half-way down a lot of the time at me, and I pulled the s**t out of him. I reached a hundred off his bowling once when he played for Sussex, whereupon he banged the next one in short and I pulled it for six. "Moley, Moley, Moley, why do you always do that to me?" he cried. "Cos you keep bowling short at me," I smiled back at him.

In the match at Taunton, Jones bowled me a bouncer and I pulled it for four. After the next ball, which was on a length and required a defensive stroke, someone in the middle shouted "Pop". I thought to myself "Who the hell said that?" It turned out to be Twosey at the non-striker's end. Mallender then came in for the next over and bowled a bouncer. "Pop," shouted Twosey again, with a big smile on his face. The umpire, Peter Willey, and Twosey didn't get on, so he said to Twosey: "Hey shut up, stop it." After another delivery, Twosey shouted "Pop" again, and I walked down the wicket and said, "What are you doing, Twosey?" He replied loudly, so that everyone in the ring and slips could hear: "Moler, they've got pop guns, but we've got cannons." Willey told him to shut up again, but I saw a couple of Somerset fielders sniggering which amused me.

Roger Twose & Peter Willey

When he was fielding, Twosey would often go back to the dressing-room for a pee for a couple of overs, which really irked Willey as he thought he was taking the piss out of him. But Twosey really did have a weak bladder. The following year when we turned up at Fenner's for an early season game against Cambridge University, Willey said to me: "Moler, we've finally got Twosey; we've passed a regulation whereby you can't go off the field unless you've got a medical exemption." But Twosey, I don't know how, had heard this was coming and had gone to the doctor and got a medical note saying that he had a weak bladder and must be allowed off mid-session." Willey absolutely blew a fuse. It was just perfect comic timing, not at Cambridge but later in the season. Willey declared he'd never in all his career had to go off. Willey told someone to tell Twosey that he couldn't go off, but Roger came over with his letter. It was very funny.

Nellie the Elephant

Another time at Fenner's, in 1992, I'd got a few and was still batting when a well-known song suddenly blared out from some speakers in the open window of a building overlooking Fenner's. "Nellie the Elephant packed her trunk and said goodbye to the circus, Off she went with a trumpety trump, Trump trump trump." Everyone thought this was hilarious. I didn't realise at first what was going on but the song was played intermittently for about 15 to 20 minutes but only whenever I was on strike or running between the wickets. Willey, who was umpiring, thought it was so funny and was not slow to let me know the music was aimed at me. I must admit I saw the funny side of it although it probably affected my concentration because I got out soon after, missing out on a hundred against the students. In fact, I never got one in the university matches, which had first-class status in those days.

Andy Lloyd

Andy and I had a bit of strange relationship; I'm not sure what it was all about. I have my suspicions. I came along as young 'Johnny Upstart' and started scoring more runs than he did after his injury. I don't think he quite liked someone new coming in and taking some of the limelight as an opening batter. We used to have a bit of a dust-up from time to time, but I wouldn't back down if I thought I was in the right. It's black and white with me; there are no grey areas. Sometimes I got into a pickle that I'd have done well not to get involved in.

In 1990 I got 1,669 championship runs and thought I would be in with a very good chance of getting 'player of the year'. It was the year of small seam, though, and Tim Munton, who had bowled very well to claim 75 wickets at 27 apiece, got the award. "It was easier to bat than bowl," Lloyd, while explaining the rationale behind his decision, said. I couldn't resist chirping back: "So that's why you only scored 646 runs if it was easier to bat?" There was always some niggle behind the scenes with him. Rightly or wrongly, I just felt that way with Lloydy.

I felt for him, though, when we went down to Hampshire, where his nemesis Malcolm Marshall was taking the new ball. It was Marshall who had hit him on the temple on his Test debut, forcing him to retire hurt with concussion and blurred vision which prevented him from playing again in that 1984 season. Lloydy asked me to take first ball, and I said "No problem." I soon tucked one away for a single, and Mashall then hit him first ball straight in the box. Lloydy went down and exclaimed, "Maco, will you fucking leave me alone?" In his latter years, Lloydy became a lot freer, staying leg side of the ball and flaying it over offside. He and Bob Cottam did a great job turning us around from a side happy with draws to winning games. He also did good things as chairman of cricket. But when we opened the batting together, it wasn't the relationship I had with Nick Knight or Roger Twose.

Keith Piper & Paul Smith

In those halcyon trophy-winning years in the 1990s, if anyone was having a rough time away from the game, we just picked it up, shared it and helped each other. We had a real good vibe in our dressing-room. We weren't afraid to become vulnerable because we knew our team-mates would support us. That's a wonderful thing, if you get that camaraderie. When the exposé about Paul Smith came out, I opened the paper one Sunday morning and saw the sex, drugs and rock'n'roll double-page spread about him. We suspected something was going on, but we didn't know quite what. We knew Paul was a wild child but didn't know he was doing drugs. So when I read the story about him, I went straight to the ground.

All the boys were there early, too, and were asking each other what the hell had been going on. Tim Munton, Dermot Reeve and Bob

Woolmer, the management team, had gone even earlier to the ground for a crisis meeting and announced there would now a drugs test for everyone. "What?" we all said. "Let's get on with it," was the majority response, but one or two were not so keen. It duly transpired that Keith Piper tested positive for cannabis use, which is now common knowledge. Munts and I were asking ourselves, "Have we been sleeping under a rock all this time?" We had no idea whatsoever this was going on. We hadn't even entertained the thought. However, we all closed ranks to try and support Pipes. He had been a silly boy, but we asked him what we could do to help him. He wasn't ostracised in any way although the club fined him and he got a ban. He was one of our teammates, so we tried to make life as comfortable as possible while this scrutiny was going on. We loved Pipes for the cheeky, chirpy rascal he was, as well as being a wonderful gloveman.

Imran Khan

At the end of my first season in the side, we were playing our final championship match on a cold September day at Edgbaston against Sussex. Imran Khan, who had his tail up after making a fine hundred on the first day, took the new ball and was bowling quickly. He produced one of those trademark balls of his that came back sharply into the right-hander. It hit me on the fleshy part of my inside right thigh, where I had no protection. I collapsed in agony. The pain was excruciating. It took me about five minutes before I was ready to face the next ball. Well, bugger me, the next one nipped back and hit me on exactly same spot. I went down like a sack of potatoes, crying out this time, I'm not ashamed to admit. The pain was off the scale, and I somehow soldiered on to reach fifty that day. I also collected a bruise that looked like Joseph's techni-coloured dreamcoat and extended from the top of the inside thigh to my knee. All the Sussex boys and Imran thought it very funny. The first thing I did was to go out and buy an inside thigh pad. I hadn't acquired one initially as I thought it would make running between the wickets difficult, but you get used to it. The other thing I recall from that match was a six that Imran hit. He was on 30 or 40, knocking it around and playing beautifully. He then played and missed at one Norman Gifford turned. Unabashed, he came down the wicket to his very next ball and hit it not into the stands but over the old Edgbaston pavilion and into the road behind it. It was eventually retrieved from the park behind it. It is one of the biggest hits I've ever seen.

Malcolm Marshall

People always ask who was the quickest of the great overseas fast bowlers like Imran, Akram and Marshall. When you get up to the top end there's not much between them. The best story I heard about Marshall was when Kent were playing Hampshire, and the teams were in the bar having a beer after the first day of a championship match. "I can read you, Maco," Carl Hooper told Marshall. "No you can't," came back the reply. Maco was very good at holding court with the young players and opposition bowlers. "Tomorrow, if I face you, I will call 'in' or 'out' to each ball you bowl to signify which way it will move," Hooper declared. "OK," replied Marshall, "we'll see how we go." So the next morning, just as Marshall was letting go of the ball after Hooper had seen the seam position, Hooper exclaimed 'Out' or 'In,' ignoring balls that were leaving him but playing those that were not. I've been been told this story by numerous people so am sure it's true. After several correct calls against Marshall, Hooper proffered 'Out', playing no shot, and then 'Oh fuck' as his off stump was sent flying by a ball that came back. Maco never verballed you, he just hissed his teeth at you.

Courtney Walsh

Courtney Walsh would run in all day and demolish the tail. Just like AD. I remember an eventful game at Cheltenham in 1996 when Walsh took 11 wickets in the match to give them an innings victory. Gloucestershire had scored 569, what was then the highest total in matches between us and them. Matt Windows scored 184, having been given out in the eighties but recalled by umpire Dickie Bird. He'd been run out but Dickie decided Mike Burns, who was keeping for us, had made two attempts to break the stumps and that Windows was in by the time he had finally dislodged the bails. When we batted, needing 420 to save the follow-on, Walsh took three quick wickets including mine to reduce us to 137 for four.

In came Anurag Singh, a very talented young stroke-player who only had to see off a few balls from Walsh, who was at the end of his spell. Singh, though, got out early on, trying to play some audacious shot off Walsh, who carried on and took six for 26 to condemn us to following on. Munts asked me to take Anurag for a walk around the ground at Cheltenham and ask him to think about game management and the interests of the team. I got 30 yards and realised it was a waste of time. Anurag declared Walsh wasn't good enough to keep him quiet and that he thought he could dominate him. Anurag didn't get picked again that year, and although he was on the staff for another three seasons he was only a fringe player. He then went into law – a good decision on his part as I'm told he's done very well – but he was a good example of a wonderfully gifted batsman who didn't quite crack on.

Mike Gatting

The first time I met Gatt was when he was England captain and there was a Test match at Edgbaston. I was a youngster on the staff in my first or second year, and they called me in to do twelfth man duties. I thought I'd get there early as I didn't want to walk into the England dressing-room, which in those days was full of people like Botham, Lamb and Gower. So, after arriving, I sat in the corner, and waited for the team to turn up. I heard this commotion on the other side of the dressing-room, but I didn't know which players had arrived as I couldn't see over the the back of a bench that was in the middle of it. Alan Oakman came round to my corner and asked me how I was. Then Gatt appeared, whereupon Oakman said, "We've got you a twelfth man called Moler who's chunky like you, Gatt." He replied, "Leave him alone, Oaky; he'll do for me. Hello, Moler, just call me Mike or captain. Enjoy the day. You're nobody's slave so don't get running around after all of them. The main thing is just to be around to help with warm-ups and stuff like that. If you get on the field, good luck."

I later got to know Gatt well and became very friendly with him through playing indoor cricket. We had a team of pros playing in an indoor league one winter – Dave Leatherdale, Dominic Ostler, Asif Din, Paul Taylor, Munts and Glad. In the first year we struggled, but in the second we won it. We used a yellow indoor ball, which was not rock hard but, if it hit you, you knew about it. After becoming mates in this league, I'd stay at Gatt's place in London when Warwickshire played Middlesex in the championship at Lord's. We'd have a lovely dinner and just talk nonsense really. He'd pull out a very nice bottle of red wine from somewhere in the depths of his house. The next morning, we'd go to the ground early and Nancy, the legendary chef at Lord's, would cook us a full English breakfast. Both the Warwicks and Middlesex boys knew we were mates, especially Phil Tufnell.

Phil Tufnell

In the 1993 season we were playing Middlesex at Edgbaston in mid-July when we made the mistake of preparing a slow turning pitch. They had gained a first innings lead of 150, and we were battling hard to stay in the game. Jason Ratcliffe, who had made a very good 82 in our first innings, and I had put on fifty for the first wicket in the second dig and were battling hard to keep out their spinners, Tufnell and John Emburey. Tuffers was bowling beautifully and got the ball on a piece of string. He was going past the edge of the bat with people around it. I'd tried to come down the wicket but he was bowling well, and I was really struggling against him. I started joking with Gatt, but Tuffers said: "Hey, stop talking with our captain, you fat f***er." Tufnell then started a new over but the ball slipped out of his hand and went to mid-wicket. I asked the umpire if I was within my rights to go and hit that ball. Tuffers shouted at me: "Don't you effing dare." I responded: "Umpire, could you instruct the bowler to go back to where he was before he let go of the ball?"

Meanwhile, I could hear Gatt behind me say, "Don't do it, Moler, don't do it please." Tufnell was now starting to get angry, shouting, "Stop talking to him, Gatt. Look at you, you two fatties together." He was still standing half-way between where the ball was on edge of the square at mid-wicket and where he should be by the popping crease. I announced, "I want to hit that ball," and Gatt again pleaded, "Oh, Moler, please don't, please don't do it." But I continued, saying: "Umpire, please instruct Philip to go back to where he bowled, and that fielder that has moved, I think I'm right in saying he must go back to where he was before." I was still thinking whether or not to hit this stationary ball. Tufnell, though, made up my mind as he'd blown a gasket and was effing and blinding. It was too good an opportunity to upset a player who was potentially a match-winning threat. So I said, "I want that ball." As I walked towards it, I was thinking I was a long way out of my crease, so I couldn't mess this up. There was a man out on the sweep but no one at cow corner. So I aimed there and stood over the ball to hit it like I would a very long putt. Thankfully I timed it perfectly and the ball sped to the mid-wicket boundary for four runs. All the crowd were cheering, and Tufnell was beside himself, calling me a fat f***er again. I replied, "Philip, please, you know it's in the rules." Gatt now chipped in saying, "Moler, leave it alone, stop it."

Tufnell still had to finish his over, and after I had nurdled a single off his next ball he produced a beauty that turned to brush Ratters' edge on the way through to the keeper. Ratters, as was his right, waited for the umpire to give him out, which he eventually did. Tufnell hurled abuse at him for waiting for the decision and had to be restrained by his teammates. He had a right go at Gatt, moaning "You support your mates before you support me." Gatt responded: "Take your cap, Tuffers, get off the field and don't come back till you've calmed down." I'd got him out of the attack briefly, but he came back twenty minutes or so later. Gatt had a go at me in a nice way and let me know he was not happy, but I repeated that it was within the rules and that I had to knock Tufnell off his rhythm. When Tufnell came back, Gatt shouted in a stern voice 'Have you calmed down now, Philip?" Back came the reply: "Yes I've calmed down, but you're still two fatties." When he bowled again, he didn't have the same rhythm, picking up only one more wicket, that of Donald, and it was Embury who cleaned us up, with six wickets, to win them the game.

Derek Underwood

I only played against him once: in 1986 at Folkestone in an extraordinary game we lost by an innings. We'd batted first and made 267, of which I topscored with 82. 'Deadly' bowled 32 overs in that innings, taking two for 48, but I managed to keep him out before falling to Eldine Baptiste. When Kent batted, Norman Gifford bowled a marathon spell, returning the remarkable analysis of 49.5-15-96-5 to claim his 2,000th first-class wicket. Kent still got a lead of 95, though, and by the time we began our second innings the pitch had crumbled and was tailor-made for Underwood. He took the new ball and bowled virtually unchanged to return the scarcely believable figures of seven for 11 from 35.5 overs. We were eventually bowled out for 65 after 76.5 overs. Paul Smith, who opened, and I blocked it for ten or twelve overs but we didn't get a run as Deadly was getting it to bounce past our shoulders. It was an unbelievable display by him, a treat to experience the legend and how he used to bowl. It was quick – he bowled very quickly for a spinner, which surprised me. Kent's close catching was superb, with Chris Cowdrey taking five catches to follow his century with the bat. I got out to Dickie Davis, the left-arm spinner who took the other three wickets and would later play for Warwickshire in 1994 and 1995 before dying tragically young, aged 37, due to cancer.

Mark Robinson

I never saw Allan Donald get really upset and lose it, but one time where he came close was in 1991 when we were playing Yorkshire at Headingley. We had got them nine wickets down in the first innings and were all huddled in the middle, congratulating Tim Munton, who has just got Stuart Fletcher out. For some reason AD had stayed down at long leg in front of where the old dressing-rooms used to be before the ground was reconfigured. Out down the steps walked Yorkshire's number eleven and complete rabbit, Mark Robinson, who was met by AD as he stepped onto the playing area. AD walked in alongside Robinson for about 40 yards, wagging his finger at him and talking to him, but we didn't know what was going on. Munts completed his over, and AD, who had bowled the previous one, was visibly impatient to start the next one and have a go at Robinson from around the wicket. I was at short leg and couldn't resist taunting Robinson: "He's nasty is Donald, he's out to get you." With his first ball AD hit Robbo straight on the white rose crest of his helmet. Down he went, and AD came down the wicket and stood over him, berating him. "Calm down, he's number 11, mate," someone said. AD's next ball whizzed straight past Robinson's chin. The umpire stepped in and said that was two bouncers for the over, with no more allowed. The next delivery was another short one into the ribs. "Hey, AD, what's going on?" Dermot questioned. AD then pitched one up from over the wicket to Robinson who, retreating onto the back foot well before the ball had been bowled, was plumb lbw. As we walked off, someone asked, "What was all that about, Al? We've never seen you do that before." The reply came back: "Two years ago when I played a second eleven match against Yorkshire, he peppered me and abused me. I never forget." Poor old Robbo; he got it back twice as bad as he must have dished it out.

AD had an extraordinary record against Yorkshire, who did not like batting against him. In that match he took five wickets in both innings to win us what was a tight game – by only 30 runs. The day before, we had beaten them by the narrowest margin I can recall in my county career – by two runs in a Sunday League match which was sandwiched in between the championship encounter. I remember another Sunday League game against them at Headingley when AD was bowling so quickly that they were taking byes to the keeper as he was standing 30 yards back. They did this for about three or four overs, and it threw us as we didn't know what to do. The keeper was so far back, but couldn't keep with a glove off as AD was bowling so fast. So he had to whip his glove off after taking the ball and throw at the stumps but the non-striker was always making his ground.

Daily Telegraph

I used to get the Telegraph every morning as it covered every first-class match, and I liked to read each match report to glean any information on opposition bowlers, especially those we were playing the next week. I found that a great help. There was one occasion, though, when I was not best pleased with one report mid-way through a championship game in my last season with Warwickshire where I was at the crease for a long time. Due to my diabetes, I had to have a sandwich with the right filling brought out for me to eat during a drinks break. Charles Randall, who was covering the match for the Telegraph, saw this but was unaware of my diabetes and made slightly unkind reference to my large appetite and physique in his report the next day. I was not very amused. The winter before, while first working with Free State in South Africa, I had been diagnosed with diabetes after feeling acute dizziness and raging thirst. Since then, I've had to inject myself four times a day with insulin.

David Thorne

Warwickshire Old Players Association have a lunch at their annual golf day where they honour an ex-player, and in 2022 it was me they honoured. A lot of former players were there like David Thorne and Paul Booth, as well as others who'd played with me. Dennis Amiss came over to them and said, "We don't see guys like you very often," whereupon Thorney, nodding at me, replied: "We've come to see him, not to see you lot. We've come to celebrate with Moler. We're not interested in the rest of you." He was quite blunt Thorney, but I was very touched.

Tribute

by Allan Donald

Warwickshire & South Africa cricketer

For me, Moler was the hard man from Coventry. It was amazing how quickly we hit it off after he picked me up from Heathrow airport when I first joined Warwickshire. He told me I was coming to one of the great clubs in the UK during the two-hour drive to Birmingham, when we had a really nice chat about everything. I was young and just looking forward to getting out, and Moler took me under his wing a little bit and got me in touch with Geoff Humpage as well. Those two were an amazing pair, looking after a young Afrikaans-speaking boy from Bloemfontein.

Moler never looked for any excuses. He was a tough guy who revelled in confrontation, loved a niggle and thrived on it with that hardness of his. He was a real competitor, an unbelievably good mate and a really good team man. We talk about guys who look after their team-mates, and he was absolutely one of them. He stirred the fire from short leg when I or Gladstone were bowling. He was a funny, typically hard-nosed Coventry guy, who pissed opponents off.

I remember ringing him in 2020 at the start of Covid to see how he was. I never knew he was about to go under the knife. I said, "How ya doing?" and he replied, "I'm good, mate. Just about to go into theatre and lose my leg." Just like that. I went "Wow" and was shocked. Not once has he complained. For him, life is life and has got to carry on. That's just Moler – he is such a great guy.

11

Free State and Hansie Cronje

Bob Woolmer had taken me aside in the 1994 season and asked me what I was going do when I finished playing. I replied that I didn't know. "Why don't you become a coach?" he questioned. "You should start your coaching courses now, so that when you finish you've got them all behind you, and you can move onto your next career." So it was thanks to Bob's encouragement that I did my level 1, level 2 and level 3 in England, then my Level 4 in South Africa in 1998/99 when I was coaching Free State. Level 4 for me was a week away in South Africa, but in England it's evolved into something like a degree – they do it over three years. You have to do modules online, and you go in for a week's residential at Loughborough. It's a good thing; there's a lot of people doing it now. Gordon Lord drew it all up, so we can thank him for putting all that together in England. Anton Ferreira set up level 4 in South Africa. Everyone used to copy the Australian way twenty years ago – everyone wanted their cricket to be the same as the Aussie way because they were the best, but people got too obsessed with it and lost a bit of ID. In the coaching world everyone wanted to introduce their own brand of cricket, with their own coaches teaching that brand. Anton did a tour of the country, talking to coaches, captains and international players, drew up what was the South African way of cricket and applied that to his thinking when he put together the level 4 course.

By the middle of the 1996 season, I was thinking seriously about coaching as a post-playing career. At the end of it, Free State invited me to come out in the 1996/97 winter for a couple of months to work with the second team. 1997 was my benefit year, and in the middle of it Free State asked me to come back and coach the first team in the 1997/98 winter. I said to them it must be a five-year deal, not a two-year one as it would mean ending my county career aged 36 when I could have carried on for another year or two. When Free State agreed to give me a five-year contract, I took the job and said my goodbyes to Warwickshire and England at the end of the 1997 season. In my final innings for the club, against Essex at Chelmsford, I ruptured my Achilles for a second time while batting with Nick Knight after he called me for a quick single. We were only chasing 43 to win and had made 40 of them when I sustained the injury. That was the end of August, and I missed the last three championship games.

So, sadly, there was no valedictory appearance for me, and I also missed the NatWest Trophy Final when we lost to Essex. In the semi-final against Sussex at Edgbaston, I'd chipped in with a fifty out of our massive total of 342, which proved far too much for the opposition. The match carried over into the reserve day which might have been a problem for Allan Donald, who was due to catch a flight back home that evening to receive South Africa's highest sporting honour, the Gold Medal of Merit, from President Mandela. Knowing time was tight, AD was irresistible with the ball, bowling like lightning to take five for 37. He just caught the flight thankfully. He returned to England to become the 19th bowler to claim 500 first-class wickets for Warwickshire in the same match I ruptured my Achilles. He was nothing short of a heroic overseas performer for the county.

I wondered if I would miss playing, but I didn't as I had been suffering from a bit of pain in the left ankle even before I did the Achilles. I was also still in a dressing-room environment at Free State, which is what players miss on retirement. We had a lot of big names but they were away a lot of the time: Hansie Cronje, Boeta Dippenaar, Nicky Boje and Donald. I worked with some good 21-year olds, and what I've become known for is helping to develop young batsmen, a good crop of which we had got into the side. I found that wherever I've gone I've enjoyed mentoring younger players, which ironically has led to my downfall. A lot of senior players took exception to it in some places: Scotland, for example, where the senior players felt their days were numbered because I was pushing younger players. This wasn't the case; I just wanted the best for them and what they could do for the team. One or two felt under pressure. Bob Woolmer used to tell me that players who are not under pressure are never going to produce their best cricket. Steve Waugh used to say that if you're friends with everyone you're not doing your job properly.

AD became an even bigger mate while I was with Free State in South Africa. My wife Jacqui and his wife Tina were quite close, and we'd have braais at each other's houses in Bloemfontein. AD was a great socialiser; he drinks as quick as he bowls. He likes a lager, is great company and never ever brags about anything he's done. Half a dozen of us would go and play golf on a day off in Bloemfontein after meeting up at about 10 or 11am. It wasn't for many months that I found out that AD, when in England, had regularly gone on off-days to the athletics track at Birmingham University to do 400-metre sprints and two-kilometre time trials. Tina would take a stop watch and send the times back to a sprint coach in South Africa that Bob Woolmer had set AD up with. He was one hell of an athlete and one of the best quick bowlers in the world, if not THE best. For me he was in the top five of all time, at least the ones I've seen live. He knew he had to look after his body, playing back-to-back seasons in England and South Africa. He brought the concept of an ice bath into our dressing-room; it was fun trying to get some of the guys into it. He started that after reading that the Australians were doing it.

When I went to Free State as coach, all I could do was check his rhythm which he asked me to look at. He wouldn't over-bowl himself and was very astute. More than once, Hansie, our team captain, would come to me at tea and say, "Talk to your quick bowler, will you?" I replied: "He's your quick bowler, not mine." Hansie countered, "He doesn't want to bowl; he says his feet are sore." So I went to see AD and, sure enough, his feet were very sore, with plasters all over them.

Free State won the plate in my first year, but thereafter we were up and down. We had a season when we did really well but lost our cohesion when the seniors came back. It sounds strange, but we just lost our momentum. At times AD wanted to rest between Test matches and was often saying, "I'm getting tired, Moler." Hansie would say to me to "get your mate to bowl, we need a spell after tea on the third day." I used to have to cajole him to bowl. One thing about Allan was that he'd turn a game in four overs. But if it was flat and hot and he thought the game was going nowhere, quite understandably he'd want to take a rest and get someone else to bowl. Hansie, being the competitor he was, would try and throw everything at a game to win it.

Hansie was magnificent to work with. He had lots of diaries, ten to fifteen of them in his coffin. It was a daily tour report: how hot the weather, what the conditions and pitch were like; who bowled well, who batted well; how he felt. Every day's play. He'd go back and read them before data came in. Who'd played well in whichever conditions. He led from the front, and players loved him as he motivated them. He'd go for a run in 40ºC and come back drenched, have a shower before having a net and then bowl. The only technical work I did with him was after a Test series versus Australia when they bounced him out. "What do I do, Moler?" he asked me. I got the bowling machine out, started with tennis balls and got him to bob and weave. He used to stay one side of it and get into trouble. I got him so he could get inside the line. Playing quick bowling is all about confidence, backing yourself – you don't have to be a good hooker and puller. If they bowl short at you, they're just not going to get you out. If a bowler doesn't think he's going to get you out, he's not going to waste his time thundering in and bowling half-way down the wicket. It just takes too much energy out of you. Hansie was a magnificent player of spin; he'd slog-sweep so well. Players wanted to do well when he was around as the national captain.

I was very surprised by the infamous match-fixing scandal involving Hansie and the Indian bookmaker. The storm broke just after South Africa returned home from a tour of India in April 2000 via a one-day tournament in Sharjah. Sacks of mail immediately came flooding into the office for him at Free State, hundreds and hundreds of letters. When I first saw him, I asked him, "Did you do it?" He said, "No, coach." Before the start of the King Commission, which was set up in Cape Town to investigate the match-fixing allegations, I asked Hansie again. "I didn't do it, coach," he said again. My only criticism is that when he had breakfast with his father on the morning of his departure to Cape Town, he told him he didn't do it, and then a few hours later at the commission he confessed on the stand that he had been "less than honest" and had accepted cash from an Indian bookmaker in Joburg on the eve of the one-day series with England and Zimbabwe, before touring India. He was in turmoil because he had two people who advised him in his life, telling him to do different things: first, a very good lawyer in Bloemfontein, who told him not to admit to anything as they hadn't released the tapes. To this day they haven't been made public. He told Hansie to make them build a case against him. Then there was his pastor, Ray McCauley, a happy-clappy evangelical type, who told him he must be clean in the face of the Lord. Hansie was very religious and fought with that. I asked him why he had eventually confessed, and he replied that he had to do the right thing by God. He had been in between a rock and a hard place. He had only got caught when the policeman, who recorded the tapes, was investigating another fraud case and was listening back to them at home. His son came in and asked him why he was listening to Hansie Cronje. The policeman said "Who?" The son replied the South African cricket captain.

In the end Hansie fell on his own sword. I don't agree with what he did but he was not an arrogant person, and he tried to help the disadvantaged people in Bloemfontein. I saw him with bags and bags of Adidas clothing that he gave away. People would queue up at the ground on the last day of a match and would come forward one by one. He'd sign an autograph and give them t-shirts, shoes and sweat shirts, all brand new in the wrapper. He had a great heart, a lovely, lovely heart. I had played against him for Griquas against the University of Free State team when he was their 20-year old captain. I also came up against him when he was at Leicestershire and got to know him through Gordon Parsons, who married Hansie's sister, Hester. They live up in the north of South Africa. The whole story with Hansie I find it very, very sad. What he did doesn't tarnish what I thought of him as he did a lot of good things, especially for South African cricket. I don't think his fatal flight crash was suspicious, as he was booked on another from Joburg to George where he lived. It got cancelled, and as he had friends in the freight industry he got a lift on the jump seat of a cargo plane. It came into George in foggy conditions, the pilot aborted the landing and turned into the mountain instead of out to sea. There was no way anyone could have known he would be on that plane. Nevertheless, Jimmy Adams, who was captain of Free State when I left them, said to me: "Coach, there were a lot of happy cricketers after that accident." I didn't ask him why, but that's why there were conspiracy theories. I was in Zimbabwe on a golf tour at the time.

That five-year period with Free State was good for me; I learnt a lot from Hansie and about dealing with cricketing politics. There was one incident, in particular, with Ray Jennings, whose son Keaton later played a few Tests for England. Ray was coach of Eastern Transvaal, and during a team meeting the day before a first-class match against Free State at Benoni in February 2001 we heard he had offered money to any of his pace bowlers who hit Allan Donald on the head. Well, AD did get hit on the head – by Andre Nel – and had to go to hospital to get checked out. The United Cricket Board held an inquiry and asked me to file a complaint against Jennings. I made it as I felt I had to; his actions were just not in the spirit of the game. Jennings was summoned to a disciplinary hearing and charged with bringing the game into disrepute. He threatened he would sue me for defamation, but one of the Eastern Transvaal players present at the team meeting, an ex-Free State player as it happened, said he would confirm what Jennings had said. When Jennings publicly stated that "an offer made in jest was perhaps taken seriously by certain of the younger players" and that he regretted any misinterpretation, the hearing was cancelled.

The matter didn't end there though – for me, at least. Bizarrely the Free State chairman then wanted to discipline me for saying people couldn't bowl bouncers at AD. Of course, I responded I hadn't meant that at all. The whole affair blew up into quite a big thing; it was debated on SA radio in the morning. It was quite a few strange, if not, crazy days. The chairman wanted to fire me as he claimed I'd brought Free State into ill repute.

Managing players, rather than officials, was more straightforward. I didn't always get it right. but I did manage to bring on a group of young players: Johan van der Wath, who went on to play to play for South Africa; Morne van Wyk, too; Boeta Dippenaar, who was only 20 when I started there; and Dewald Pretorius, who played for Warwickshire and the Proteas, having come from a terrible background after being orphaned very young. He would come down to bowl in exchange for a can of Coke. He improved and improved, and we signed him. Free State was where I first came across a youthful Matthew Hoggard, who Corrie van Zyl had brought over from England to play club cricket and act as a paid net bowler. Corrie went off to be South Africa coach, and

I took over at Free State. I saw Hoggard swinging it round corners, so I went to my boss and asked if we could pick him. The answer was no. I put up with this for about two weeks but went back and said, "This cannot go on any more. This kid is too good; he's got to play." I got my wish, and on his one-day debut for us his first wicket was Jonty Rhodes, lbw. He ran down the wicket shouting "Jonty F***ing Who." He ended up doing very well for us, and his time at Free State really developed his bowling. England were over that season, and I rang Bob Cottam, formerly Warwickshire's coach who was now England's bowling coach, and asked him if he'd seen this Hoggard and if he would have him down to bowl in the England nets. After seeing Hoggard, Cottam rang me and said, "Bloody hell, we need to keep an eye on him." England, for their part, helped him a lot with his training programmes.

In the South African winter I'd travel all over the state to quite remote Free State settlements like Bethlehem, Clarens, Ladysmith and areas like that, and get the schoolteachers together to run a basic level 1 or 2 course to help them coach the kids. Nico Pretorius, a pace bowler who played over 50 first-class matches for Free State, came with me, too. I'd make sure the players not going away had a winter programme with nets twice a week and one-on-ones. My kids used to play football at Grey College, a top private school, and I used to referee. White boys had boots, but the African boys played barefoot but with such passion, which was magnificent to watch. It was 15 minutes each way, and I'd tease my sons I'd send them off, especially Matthew the younger one who was a little terror, running around tackling. The older one was in goal. Every Friday night, I'd have a braai at home, and on Saturday I'd run around as ref regretting the night before. I found the winter was when you actually did most of your coaching work, looking closely at techniques. I was quite close to Nicky Boje, who was frustrated for a long time as he couldn't get in the national side. I helped him with his batting but got bowling coaches in for the bowlers. Boje eventually got his opportunity in a one-day game because he could bat. He was one of the early pinch-hitters that were successful.

I was in my second year at Free State in 1998/99 when my ex-Warwickshire team-mate Wasim Khan, who had moved to Derbyshire, came out to South Africa and stayed with me in Bloemfontein. I said I'd find an hour a day for him on the bowling machine as well as some net bowlers. He showed me the ad for the Hong Kong coaching role which was during the South African off-season, and I applied. Lo and behold, I got the job. Hong Kong was a great experience, and my first with an 'international' side. The job spec was five to six weeks in Hong Kong preparing their players for an ICC tournament in Toronto, which lasted two weeks. The players all had jobs and were a mixture of expats – Aussies, New Zealanders, Pakistanis and Indians, as well as one or two Chinese brought up in English schools. It was a real mix of cultures. They looked after me fantastically well. I was based at the Kowloon Cricket Club, which was one of two major clubs, the other one being the Hong Kong CC. The nets were artificial, and the grounds small as there was no spare land there. We would start practice as early as 5.30am as players had to be at work for 7.30 or 8am. The majority had financial services jobs. I set up two nets, each with a bowling machine. I gave them a choice – morning or evening or both – but told them they must do a minimum of three sessions a week. There would be one or two could come in the day, so I ended up having a programme for them.

What I learnt was that I needed to be better prepared next time round. I thought we had quite a useful team with one good Pakistani quick who could make a difference. But the first game we played in Toronto was on a proper-sized field with big boundaries. Thanks to their size, three of our players threw their shoulders out in the first game and couldn't bowl. They had only played in Hong Kong on postage stamps with little more than lobs needed from the boundary. That taught me I had to be proactive as a coach; thirty years ago there wasn't much forward thinking as a coach. The Hong Kong experience was something I thoroughly enjoyed, a great vibrant city. I stayed at a hotel that was a 15-minute walk from the club, which I enjoyed as I loved taking in the hustle and bustle of the streets. I've been very fortunate in my career to have travelled around the world quite a bit. I just love experiencing different cultures and seeing how different people live around the world. That's what gave me the bug if you like: about travelling with cricket to see as much of the world as I could and experience different lifestyles.

Free State, Hong Kong and, later on, Kenya were coaching jobs where I learnt a lot about how players behaved, both well and badly;

and when badly, how to deal with it. One thing Bob Woolmer instilled in me was that you don't have to win every fight, just the important ones. In other words, pick your battles. It was especially the case when I was in Kenya. Players from different cultures behave in different ways. Some react differently to discipline. The conservative Afrikaans Free Staters would thrive on discipline. If you told them they had to be at nets at 3pm, they would all be there at 2.30pm. Or at 7.30am if I told them 8am training. In Kenya, three or four players would turn up at 8.20am which really annoyed me.

The other thing that Free State taught me is bringing on young players and our success with that. We didn't win anything, but I recall Hansie telling me, "When you leave here, you shouldn't be judged on how many trophies you've got hanging in the president's boardroom but whether you leave the place better than you found it." In other words, have you brought on young players? When I went there, a lot of senior players had left and we had young 19-20 year olds. When I left, a lot of those had gone on to play for South Africa, and the ones underneath them had come through. They were left with a crop of fine young players that put them in good stead to go on and win things in the next few years.

Not only that, bringing Jimmy Adams in as the captain for my last two seasons was one of my better moves. He was a superb leader of the team, really bonding with the young players and spending time with them. I couldn't say a bad thing about him. He was a house friend and would come and have Christmas dinner with us. My kids loved him. He was just a genuinely nice man. He went on to become West Indies' director of cricket, and I still keep in touch with him. He said to me when I left, "Coach, I've been dreading this day because they've been talking to me for two weeks now about me taking over from you as player-coach for an interim period, but I said I wouldn't do it. I'll captain the side, but I'm not taking Andy Moles' job. He has been good to me. If you want to get rid of him, you do it but you're not going to do it if I'm going to be the coach." So they brought Corrie van Zyl to be the next coach. They wanted to get rid of me as the results hadn't been good enough. I was naive to think coaches weren't fired very often. I expected to see out my full contract and bring on these young players. I was quite hurt when I was moved on a couple of months into the fifth year of my contract but, looking back, I should have seen it coming, notwitstanding it was my first coaching job.

There was no cricket committee, just the board. One person on the board supported me all the time: Ewie Cronje, Hansie's father, who was a great cricket man who ran University of Free State cricket for years. He was a lovely man, a very good human being and a caring, considerate person. When I had that battle over AD being hit on the head and the chairman called a board meeting to fire me, it was Ewie who led a group of people against him, saying that I had done nothing wrong. They tried to bend him to back down but he wouldn't, and it was he and the managing director, Seppi Lusardi, who fought that off in the boardroom. It was Seppi who said I must be given my eight months' money when I was sacked after they had offered only two months. He was a fair man, Seppi; I enjoyed working for him.

As for the president of the Free State board, a strong character named Charlie Robinson, he liked to meddle in cricketing matters when unqualified to do so. He rang me once in my fourth year as coach when we had a good day: 350 for 3 at the end of the first day of four and the wicket was drying. "Good day today, coach," he said. "Hopefully we'll bowl them out tomorrow." "No, we won't, we're batting on," I replied. "No you'll declare overnight," he ordered. "No I won't," I told him. "We're going to bat on, try and get 500. The wicket will deteriorate, and we've got Nicky Boje to bowl them out." So he started demanding that we declare straightaway but I refused. He was a salt farmer with no playing experience. He'd sit with me when we were in the field, along with the physio and the twelfth man. "I know you don't think I know much about cricket," he said one day. I replied: "I haven't said that, Charlie; you're saying it, not me." By this time we had a relationship that could be a bit patchy. He then added: "I used to sit on the sidelines when I was at school and watch Graeme Pollock bat, so I do know about cricket." Dumbstruck, I said: "You're telling me that watching him bat trumps my 15 successful years of first-class cricket in England and three years as a coach out here." He said that it did. I replied: "Charlie, let's leave it there. I don't even want to have this conversation." Anyway, we batted on and did win the game.

12

Kenya

After I was sacked by Free State, I tried a little business thing with a friend of mine, selling mortgages on behalf of banks. It kept me busy but never really got off the ground. A friend ran it; he was a 60% shareholder and I was 40%. Bob Woolmer, however, had kept in touch and been appointed ICC's high performance manager, with a special responsibility for its Associate Member countries like Scotland, Ireland, Kenya and Canada. According to Bob, Kenya, after their unexpected progression to the semi-finals of the World Cup, were going to be the next Test-playing nation. Their coaching role had become vacant, and Bob said the ICC would fly me up for an interview with the Kenya board.

So, a few weeks after the World Cup final of 2003, I caught a flight up to Nairobi from Johannesburg and was interviewed by the Kenya Cricket Association there. It was run by the chairman, Sharad Ghai, an Asian like all the rest of the board. Nearly all the players, though, were Africans, which led to political problems later on. The interview went well and I was offered the job on a two-year deal. I stayed in a nice little flat in a complex in Nairobi, but getting around the city to practise was a problem. The traffic and state of the roads were terrible, and I used to warn my family not to be surprised to get a phone call saying I'd been killed in a road accident. I would spend four months up there and six weeks back home in South Africa. I drove a wreck of a car and had countless close shaves as the standard of driving was so bad. I'd come round a corner, and a lorry would be coming straight at me on the wrong side.

There were two Asians in the side, with the rest Africans of different tribes. In most games when a player reached fifty, four or five would clap but the rest would not as they were from a different tribe. They were only happy when their own tribal people did well. Maurice Odumbe, a very affluent, suave guy who liked the nightlife, was a smooth operator and got on well with everybody. Sadly, though, he got involved with match-fixing in my first year, was caught and received a lengthy ban. It was a big loss as he was our number four batter and senior pro under the captaincy of Steve Tikolo. Maurice always seemed to make things happen on the field.

I had initially walked into a massive argument between players and board. When the players left for the 2003 World Cup in South Africa, the board told them any prize money they won they could keep. They'd only expected them to win one game, maybe, but after beating Sri Lanka, Zimbabwe and Bangladesh, Kenya reached the semis, although had New Zealand not forfeited their match against Kenya in Nairobi, they would not have got beyond the group stage. Suddenly Kenya had won big prizemoney – $US 530,000 – but the board were not happy about distributing it. Prize money goes direct to boards, with most holding back a small percentage for grass roots cricket. Sharad ran the board with a rod of iron. I don't know if they were corrupt, but I was suspicious of them. As I arrived, the row was ongoing. The board tried to renegotiate, saying it wanted to retain a biggish percentage of the prize money. It got so acrimonious that the players announced they were going to go on strike and would often withdraw 24 hours before a game. I'd go to the board, and negotiations would start again. The board would say we'll sort it out by the next game but they didn't. I didn't want to get involved. I said to both parties: "Do not bring me into this. This is your fight; you sort it out." If Sharad asked my opinion I'd say, "If you've got a deal with them, then honour it." Sharad didn't like this. An interim payment was eventually made, but the players kept going after the balance.

Where it broke down for me, and what caused me to leave Kenya, was when we got to the semi-final of the ICC Intercontinental Cup, a new three-day first-class tournament between ICC Associate Member countries. This ran from March to November 2004 with Africa, the Americas, Asia and Europe forming groups with three countries in each. We topped the Africa group, seeing off Uganda and Namibia, and were due to meet Scotland, the Europe group winner, in the semi-finals in Abu Dhabi. Two days before we were due to fly, the players announced they were going on strike. I told them that the chance of playing Test cricket was there; all they had to do was win this three-day competition. "This is your big opportunity," I told them. "You need to win the battle but not today. You can fight it when you come back. If you win in the UAE, you have more ammo to have a go at the board."

But they wouldn't budge. I went to the board, who called the players' bluff by saying the Under-19 team would go instead. This threw the players, who hadn't seen that coming. The U19 team was an Asian team, apart from one or two black Africans. It did not go down well with the black Africans that a board comprising Asians was sending an Asian team to represent Kenya. I lost all respect for Steve Tikolo when he came to me and said, "You're a racist; you're backing them over us." I replied: "Hey, I live in South Africa. Do not be throwing the racist card at me. If that's what you really think, I'm done here." I told him I'd never talk to him again, and I haven't. I went with the Under-19s but they were bowled out for 95 in the first innings in reply to Scotland's 300 for five declared. The Scots declined to enforce the follow-on, and made 401 for seven declared in their second dig, ensuring they qualified for the final by dint of superior bonus points from the match. Scotland won the final in Sharjah, thrashing Canada by an innings. A month later I joined Scotland as their coach after the position was advertised and I applied. I told Sharad I was leaving, and he said he wasn't surprised but thanked me for doing a good job. It ended up an amicable parting. I had served 20 months of my two-year contract.

Kenya did improve during my time as their coach, although we didn't play enough cricket to test the team. After the 2003 World Cup high, we were brought back to earth when we lost a one-day series 5-0 at home to Sri Lanka A in October of that year. In 2004 we had both the India and Pakistan A teams over for first-class matches, in which our bowlers struggled although our batsmen did well. A month later, however, in the Champions Trophy in England, we were badly short of runs in matches against both India and Pakistan. Against the latter at Edgbaston, we collapsed from 67 for one to 94 all out in ten overs. I felt the players were far too interested in how much they'd get paid for using certain cricket bats. About four or five contacted all the batmakers, and I remember one banging on about how one would give him 50 dollars if he used their bat in a game. They were totally driven by how much money they could make. I understood why, but they weren't concentrating on preparing for a game the next day. They needed to compartmentalise it and try to get deals on off days, but not on practice days. I'd say, "Guys, forget about that nonsense. It will look after itself if you win a game or two. Then you'll get even more money."

Kenyan cricket has since gone backwards. They didn't have the right work ethic. Mark Lane, an Englishman, was my assistant and an excellent cricket coach who went on to work with the England women's team. I recruited him after meeting him in Bloemfontein. I liked the way he thought, and he fitted what both I and the team needed. He was a down-to-earth, hard-working coach. The board supported me and brought him in, although every now and then they made like difficult for him. Once, when we were off on a tour to Hong Kong, Sharad told me that Mudassar Nazar, the former Pakistani all-rounder who was coaching Kenya's Under-19s, would come in place of Lane as my assistant. I knew how much Mark had been looking forward to the tour, which was a reward for all the hard work he had put in. I told the board to tell Lane, but Nazar got wind and said he couldn't be seen working under someone who hadn't played Test cricket. He couldn't take directions from, or assist, someone who hadn't played at the level he'd played at. So Laney did get to come to Hong Kong.

Learning about dealing with difficult players is what I took from my time with Kenya. I was pig in the middle all the time, which was hard. I was disappointed the board didn't stick to the agreement over the World Cup prize money, but equally the players didn't play enough and missed their opportunities. They could have done better. With three or four regions that play against each other, they only really had 30 to 40 players in the country we could select from. Although their diets weren't great, they did get much fitter after we set up three training sessions a week and improved their running between wickets. The bowling got a lot more consistent, thanks to improved fitness, but they didn't bowl enough.

A good example was Collins Obuya, the leg-spinner who was signed by Warwickshire after the World Cup on the basis of one good performance of five for 24 against Sri Lanka. I was sceptical when I watched him bowl in Kenya as he was so erratic, and it came as no real surprise his brief time in county cricket was a disaster. He spent most of his three months at the county in the second team, claiming three wickets at 60 apiece in his two championship appearances before returning home early with a knee injury. Steve Perryman, the Warwickshire second-eleven coach of the time, rang me exasperated one day and quipped, "From a country that's produced some of the world's greatest middle-distance runners, we've been sent a Kenyan who can't even run 22 yards."

My three brothers Paul, Simon and Mark; the Silver Jubilee –
me (far right) with my brothers, mum and grandma.

With Tony Finch and Gladstone Small; Finchy and Tim Munton at Tim's wedding.

Teaching my boys the basics!

Fresh-faced in 1987.

Celebrating the NatWest Trophy win in the Lord's dressing room in 1995; acknowledging the applause for my hundred in the NatWest semi-final against Kent in 1994.

Dermot Reeve strumming his guitar at Canterbury where we clinched the County Championship in 1995; Roger Twose, Dominic Ostler and I celebrate with the Sunday League trophy in 1994.

With New Zealand skipper Daniel Vettori; giving some advice to Dawlat Zadran when I was Afghanistan coach.

Taking a break....

13

Scotland

Kenya was a finishing school for my personal development as a coach. I started to put two and two together quicker than I did at Free State, where I was a bit naive. I could not wait to start with Scotland, where I arrived in early 2005 on an 18-month contract, which was extendable if we qualified for the 2007 World Cup in West Indies. I lived in a beautiful two-bedroom flat in Edinburgh, near the city centre, and loved it there.

The 2005 season went quite well, with the highlight a victory over Warwickshire in Stratford-on-Avon in division 2 of the 45-over totesport Sunday League. We had a good crop of talented club cricketers, that were reinforced by two overseas players: Yasir Arafat, a quality Pakistani pace bowler who did a great job for us, and a young lad from Free State called Jonathan Beukes, whom we didn't have to pay much as he was already playing Scottish league cricket for Stenhousemuir. I was obviously keen to put one over my old county and, after putting them in, we reduced them to 17 for five to the consternation of a 3,500 home crowd watching Warwickshire's inaugural one-day game at the pretty Swans Nest Lane ground. We bowled them out for 113 and were cruising to our target at 70 for one. Somehow we slipped to 108 for nine before last man Paul Hoffman, who had earlier taken three for 19, smashed Neil Carter over extra cover for six. The Edinburgh-based Caledonian Brewery, who had a tent on the boundary for the day, celebrated Scotland's win by reducing the cost of a pint to £1, and quite a few of our players took advantage. I didn't know then that Warwickshire's coach John Inverarity, the former Australia Test player, was going at the end of the season. He was a gentleman who was very gracious in defeat. For me it meant a lot to beat my old county but looking back it was just another game. At the time I thought it more important than it really was. I wanted to coach Warwickshire one day and thought, wrongly or rightly, that winning that game would put me in good stead.

Warwickshire weren't the only county we beat that summer in the totesport League. We succeeded at Taunton, where Australia had failed two days previously, in overcoming Somerset by 15 runs after setting them 233. Beukes played very well for his 92 before Arafat took three for 33 from his nine overs. Disappointingly that day, however, Asim Butt, our opening bowler and comfortably the oldest player in the side at 37, failed a drugs test for cannabis. He confessed and was banned from cricket for a year. I really didn't have him down as a recreational drug user.

To qualify for the 2007 World Cup, we had to finish in the top five countries of the 12 that took part in the ICC Trophy in Ireland in the first half of July 2005. There were two groups of six, with the top two in each earning a semi-final spot but more importantly a place in the World Cup. The two sides finishing third in each group would play off for the fifth and final World Cup berth. We were in much the tougher group with Canada, Holland and Namibia, the three teams that had kept Scotland out of the 2003 World Cup. Also-rans Oman and Papua New Guinea were also in the group. I've no doubt we benefited from playing those totesport 45-over games against the counties earlier that summer as it gave us a hard professional edge. The tight wins against Warwickshire and Somerset, as well as a tie against Derbyshire, had given us self-belief. For we won every group game in Ireland, with only Namibia, whom we beat by 27 runs, running us close. Victory over defending champions Holland by 98 runs in our final group game clinched our World Cup spot and allowed us a big celebration in Belfast that night.

Two days later we convincingly won our semi-final against Bermuda in Dublin, chasing down a target of 220 in 50 overs with wickets and time to spare. Our old adversaries, Ireland, beat Canada in the other semi, which set up a Celtic final at Clontarf, which was televised and attended by 3,000. They had a strong side but, after putting us in on a good wicket, bowled poorly. We batted superbly to reach 324 for five, with Ryan Watson making 94 and Warwickshire all-rounder Dougie Brown 59 off 44 balls. Ireland had a young Eoin Morgan at number three and Middlesex's Ed Joyce at number four, but Hoffman, who was the leading wicket-taker in the tournament with 17, made two important breakthroughs, dismissing Morgan for 4. Joyce batted well for his 81, but Ireland finished 47 runs short. Craig Wright, our captain, was presented with the trophy, a globe on a plinth, and Ryan with the man-of-the-match award. A long night of celebration followed.

By this time, though, I knew the the Warwickshire coaching job was becoming available. I went back to Edinburgh to see Cricket Scotland's CEO, Roddy Smith, and told him I was going to apply for the Warwickshire job. He said that was fine, but that if I didn't get it Scotland would give me a new two-year deal. I heard from different sources that Dennis Amiss was not very happy with the applicants for the Warwickshire job. Amiss told Tony Finch, a Warwickshire committee member and an old mate of mine, at the NatWest final that "we might as well give the job to Moler as the others weren't up to it." Then it transpired Amiss had had a meeting with the former New Zealand Test batsman Mark Greatbatch, who was the academy coach at Edgbaston, and told him to apply. A short list of three – Greatbatch, James Whitaker and myself – was agreed on, with all of us summoned to Edgbaston for interviews with a panel. This comprised Amiss, Tim Munton, John Claughton, a committee member, and Jamie McDowell, a lawyer. Having come down from Scotland, I stayed with Munts, and in the car on the way back to his house he said that the job was provisionally mine. The panel were split 2-2 between me and Greatbatch, but that he, Munton, as chairman of cricket, would surely get the deciding vote. Before any final appointment could be announced, however, Amiss said the chairman Neil Houghton had first to be informed.

The next day Amiss revealed no contact could be made with Houghton as he was not reachable in Wales at a remote holiday cottage where there was no mobile signal. Meanwhile, the well-informed local journalist, Paul Bolton, rang Munton to say the new plan was to re-interview Greatbatch and myself with another panel. Amiss rang at end of that day to say we must be truly transparent with five on the panel, thereby precluding any chance of a deciding vote by Munts. The new panel comprised Houghton, Gladstone Small, Munton, Amiss and John Winspear, a committee member who was involved with the Under-16s.

When I went in for the second interview in front of the new panel, the first question I received was from Winspear, who asked. "What do you know about the Under-16s?" I hadn't been at the club for eight years, so I replied, "That's a strange question, John. The chairman just said I'm being interviewed for first-team coach. What do you mean what do I know about them?" He came back, "Well you need to know about the Under-16s. I mean Greatbatch is in the academy and knows all about the Under-16s."

All of a sudden I knew Winspear was a plant, and I'd now got the hump. From the very first question I knew it was a scam. It was all over for me as Amiss, Winspear and the chairman were going to vote for Greatbatch. I get emotional about this, but Amiss had said that the club couldn't have a coach who hadn't played Test cricket. Greatbatch, of course, had. They'd framed the questions to make it as easy as possible to get Greatbatch in. I walked out, went straight to the airport and flew to South Africa that night.

The next morning, when I was driving from Johannesburg airport back to Bloemfontein, I got a phone call from Amiss. "Moler, I'm sorry," he said before I interrupted him: "Dennis, just leave it. I know what you're going to say, and I don't want to hear it." I'd fallen out with him before, when he'd reneged on a pay rise promise, and now I felt he'd shafted me again. At that moment it was my dream job to go back and coach at Warwickshire, and I felt it had got taken away from me in what had been an unfair process. Munts ended up resigning as chairman of cricket on the back of Greatbatch's appointment, which was not a success as it transpired. Looking back it's still one of my great regrets I never got to coach a county in England, especially at Warwickshire, but I've rebuilt bridges with Amiss and I accept he wanted an ex-Test player.

However, the fact Greatbatch was not a success undermined Amiss's theory. He is president of the club and makes a point of coming over and shaking my hand when I go into the committee room, as well as saying I should have played for England, which makes the whole episode all the more ironic. Ten years ago he would hardly say a word to me. But he's mellowed, and I have too. I was either black or white with no middle ground. What's also ironic is that when I later left my position as New Zealand coach, they brought in Greatbatch in an interim role and he lasted one tour and a few weeks. The players wanted him out straightaway.

Once I'd missed out on the Warwickshire job, I had said to Roddy Smith in Edinburgh I wanted to take the six best young Scottish players to South Africa to be part of an academy in the Free State, playing club cricket in Bloemfontein. "Great idea," he said. However, Richard Done, who'd succeeded Bob Woolmer as high performance director at the ICC, contacted me and said the ICC would finance a three-month intake, with me as head coach and two players from each of the five associate countries that had qualified for the World Cup. It would be called an ICC high performance academy and be based at Tux University in Pretoria. Mark Lane and Bob Cottam were the assistant coaches, and the whole enterprise was a great success. Morgan was one of the two Irish selections and was just different gravy, an unbelievable talent. We played games against a Joburg league eleven, and he scored a hundred with a stick of rhubarb. You could see how talented he was, even at 19. He had a great attitude.

The academy wound up just before Christmas 2005. I spent it at home in Bloemfontein, expecting to get written confirmation of the two-year deal that had been verbally agreed would start when I got back from the academy. Worryingly I heard nothing and I rang Smith, who said the board couldn't keep me on as coach. I was flabbergasted. "The players don't want you," Smith told me. "What do you mean they don't want me?" I replied. This conversation was between Christmas and New Year, and I told him that I would fly immediately back to Scotland to meet the players one-on-one and find out what the issue was. So I flew back and fixed an hour with each player in Edinburgh, Glasgow and Aberdeen. One said they didn't know whether I was truly committed to Scotland and wondered why I hadn't bought a house. "Well, I only had an 18-month contract," was my response. "But you applied for that Warwickshire job," he shot back. Then I met Craig Wright, the captain, who from nowhere said: "This is my team, not your team. It's all about you in the press and that you're in charge, but I've built this team up."

What had happened during the ICC Trophy in Ireland was that Dougie Brown had to do a fitness test before a match mid-tournament after sustaining a strain. He made no complaints and duly passed it. Before the final I said to Craig, who had picked up a niggle in the semi and took it easy in practice the day before the final, that he too must pass a fitness test. He said he didn't need to, but I told him: "No, it's not one rule for Dougie and another for you. We need you to be right to bowl." He grumbled and wasn't happy but passed the test and took three wickets in the final. But I think he held the enforced test against me.

When I went to see another senior player, who was a very bright lawyer, he said: "Moler, you do know that Roddy has rung every single player before you meet them to instruct them to say everything's fine but that meanwhile they're working out a way to get you out." So Smith was going against me behind my back. I went to see the chairman of the Scottish Cricket Union, Keith Oliver, with whom I had had a good relationship, and told him Smith was behaving in an unbecoming manner and that the players were not being truthful with me. He said, "I'm appalled at the behaviour here and feel totally sorry for you, but they've decided they don't want you and I can't really go against that. You've done nothing wrong. It's been a power struggle with the senior players, and I'm embarrassed by their behaviour." So I packed my bags and left Scotland after only nine months as coach.

Three and a half years later, in the ICC World Twenty20 tournament in England, Scotland got drawn against New Zealand, for whom I was now head coach. Those senior Scottish players who had forced me out were still around. Before the tournament began, I took the New Zealand team to Sir Paul Getty's ground at Wormsley in Buckinghamshire for a two-week camp, where we had nets and range hitting. The players loved it as the square there has really good cricket wickets, and the setting is stunning. Meanwhile, Done suggested getting a group of associate country players together to form a composite side to play New Zealand at Wormsley. There were three Scots in it: Wright and two others. During the warm-ups on the day of the match, they came over to say hello. I said, "Hello, boys, how are you going?" Wright replied: "Coach, we're just here to apologise." I said, "What for?" He answered:

"For the way we treated you, and the way we spoke to you. We got it wrong; we're just really really sorry." I looked him in the eye and said: "I know how difficult this is for you, but ok, mate, I appreciate you coming across. It's over, it's gone. I've been fortunate to get my career going again and in a place where I thought I never would do."

We shook hands and, when we played Scotland at the Oval and beat them, they asked me over for a drink at their team hotel that evening. I went and had a few beers with the Scottish team, who had a different CEO with them. I enjoyed their company and was happy that we had buried the hatchet. As they're so proud, the Scots, and even arrogant at times about themselves and the nation, it took a lot for Craig to come and apologise like that. I respected him as a man because he did it. Peter Drinnen, a Queenslander who took over from me as coach, was already working for Scotland when I was there. I think he was probably guilty of helping my departure along so that he could get my job. At the time I was very angry but, looking back, they thought I was on a journey with them to the World Cup and they couldn't understand why I'd applied for a job in county cricket. When I went away to work with the ICC Academy in South Africa, I think that whole issue of my Warwickshire application festered between Smith and Wright.

Back in South Africa in early 2007, I'd got no job but a few months later, I received a call from the ECB. "Coach Andy Pick's having a sabbatical, and would you like to coach the England Under-19s for six weeks that summer?" was the question. I gladly accepted, but I had to pay for my own flight over which I thought was very poor from the ECB. We had some good young players, including Moeen Ali, Adam Lyth, Adil Rashid and Steve Finn, all of whom went on to play Test cricket. Rory Hamilton-Brown was captain, a very confident young man from a very wealthy family and Dennis Amiss' godson by chance. He didn't score the runs he should have done and didn't seem to want it enough. He played the way he lived. But as Bob Cottam used to say, you can't play cricket with a fur-lined jockstrap. The Kiwis refer to the need for a bit of mongrel in you, but Rory wasn't a fighter and left the professional game quite young.

We lost both the one-day and four-day 'Test' series, although the latter went to the final half hour of third Test at Shenley when we were finally bowled out with 20 minutes remaining. That gave them a 1-0 win after the first two Tests were drawn. In the opening Test at Canterbury, a young Virat Kohli scored a hundred and looked a future Test batsman. In the second Test at Taunton, Rashid, batting at number six, scored a hundred as well as taking ten wickets in the match. Varun Chopra, the Essex opener who later joined Warwickshire, also excelled with twin hundreds in the same match. I was surprised at the end of the second day when Hugh Morris of the ECB rang me to query why Rashid had bowled 18 overs in the day. I said, "Yes, in three spells of six; are you telling me 19-year olds can only bowl four-over spells?" adding that the situation of the game meant there was no other option. Moeen didn't have the control he later had, and after he failed twice with the bat in the first Test we dropped him for the remaining two. I nevertheless wrote in my end-of-series report that he would be a match-winner who could change the course of a game: 'Let him express himself, and don't over-coach him. Do not swamp him with too much technical stuff. Let him explore his natural game and freedom.'

14

New Zealand

It was thanks to Tim Munton spotting an ad for the Northern Districts coaching position that I applied after returning to South Africa in August 2006. I had two interviews online, got the job and flew to Auckland in September. Northern Districts have a big catchment area that starts an hour's drive south of Auckland around Hamilton and stretches up north of it as well, right up to Whangerei. The ground there has a lovely pavilion which is based on the Lord's one, not an exact replica but you can see the likeness. I thoroughly enjoyed my two seasons with Northern Districts, where we had a fantastic team spirit that was the closest to that of Warwickshire in our trophy-winning years. James Marshall was the captain; both he and twin brother Hamish played for New Zealand. If you put them side by side, you couldn't tell them apart. Only the shoes they wore gave them away. The team bonded well and really supported each other. James was very much like Dermot in that he was so positive around a team environment.

The season before I arrived, Northern Districts had finished bottom of the four-day State Championship, winning none of their eight games. In my first year, we turned it around completely, topping the table to earn us home advantage in the five-day final which was against second-placed Canterbury, whose coach was my mate from South Africa, Dave Nosworthy. Only needing a draw to clinch the trophy, although we didn't set out for one, I ordered a good batting wicket at Seddon Park in Hamilton. We took a wicket with the fourth ball of the match, but their second wicket pair of Michael Papps and Shanan Stewart proceeded to put on 243, laying the platform for a big total of 443 for eight declared. We slipped to 151 for five in reply and were in danger of following on, but we rallied to make 319. Papps again got runs in their second dig – 96 to follow his first innings hundred – and became the first batsman to pass 1,000 runs in a New Zealand season for six years. We were set a stiff target 374 to win on a pitch still playing well, but a draw would be enough to clinch the title. There was some iffy weather around, too.

I said to the guys, "Just don't get out. You can all bat; we bat all the way down. Just bat out time. We finished top of the table and, if we can't win the game, we've earned the right not to lose it." We lost both openers quickly enough but Alun Evans, the former Glamorgan player, and Hamish Marshall just batted and batted. My mate Nosworthy kept chiding me, saying, "Come on, give it a go", but I was never going to be tempted. Canterbury tried everything, including little loopy-loopy bowlers, but I kept telling our guys, "Just bat." Evans kept knocking it back and ground out a hundred, sharing an unbroken third wicket stand of 149 with Marshall, who made 80. We had won our first title since 1999/2000 and done a Leicester City – gone from bottom to top in one season. I told the team, "It doesn't matter what anybody thinks. You've earned it by the way you've played for the rest of the season. You finished top, and now you take your rewards."

I applied a lot of the things I'd learnt from Bob Woolmer at Warwickshire, and they bought into it. And it worked. We gelled and had a very good side, in which everyone contributed. Graeme Aldridge, who was a Munton-like back-of-a-length seamer with a mechanical run-up, was our best bowler in four-day cricket that season but suffered a very bad experience in a T20 league match against the eventual winners Auckland. With one ball left, Auckland needed 12 to win, and so had lost the match, but Aldridge bowled a full toss above waist height after slipping which was not only no-balled but hit for four by Andre Adams. That meant Auckland needed six off the last ball, and Adams smashed it out of the ground. It was a devastating loss for us.

After the match, we had to get on a bus to go to Whangerei, a five-hour drive, for an important four-day game up there. You can imagine what the dressing-room was like. There was absolute silence. There was a big long table bench in the middle of it. Everyone had their head down, and I spent a couple of minutes walking around this table, just looking at everybody, thinking 'What do I say?' I was absolutely gutted, and they were obviously gutted. So I said: "Right, if anybody says anything to Graeme about that final delivery, I will personally drag you out of this dressing room. He's bowled like a trooper all year long, he's your mate, your team-mate. You have got to support him. Do you understand me?" There were some mutterings. I continued: "Get on the bus, I'm going to put a crate of beer on it. You all have a drink on the way up there, and you do not discuss this. It's done, it's dusted. You can do nothing about it. We've got a big game in two days' time, and if we win two of the last three games, then we top the state championship. There's nothing that can be gained from pulling this apart right now. Talk about it tomorrow perhaps, but right now, leave it." Looking back, I'm proud of that speech as it had the desired effect. We did go on to win the championship, and the unfortunate Aldridge later got picked for the New Zealand one-day side.

The Auckland coach, Mark O'Donnell, was another good mate of mine as I knew him from South Africa where he had coached Transvaal. What I grew really to like about the coaching system in New Zealand was that all six provincial coaches worked together as we were all employed by New Zealand Cricket. Every spring NZ Cricket got all six coaches together for a three-day conference at their HQ. It was the idea of an Australian who was cricket director for NZ Cricket. People came in and talked about team building and tactics. On the last afternoon he asked us what new ideas we had for our own teams for the forthcoming season. I thought that I was not going to tell him what we were doing at Northern Districts, but he read my mind and declared this was where we shared ideas. I was the last one to speak. I revealed we were looking to sweep more, as well as reverse-swing the ball more. All our ideas were collated and then sent up to the national team for consideration. The way it works in New Zealand is that all the coaches are paid the same money by NZ Cricket, with your salary coming from a grant by NZ Cricket. Because of that funding, you're duty-bound to reveal all your ideas for the good of the national side. When I left the conference, I thought, "Bloody hell, there were some good ideas there." Each coach would leave with three or four ideas from the others and apply them to their respective sides.

One of the ideas that was promulgated was that bowlers must hit the stumps with the new ball. It couldn't go over them as you're then taking lbw and bowled out of play. In practice sessions bowling coaches painted a line across the pitch and seamers had to bowl on it or just the other side of it. In pre-season seamers ran in and consistently had to hit that painted line. It was the Wellington coach, an Aussie, who brought that in for his attack. Lo and behold, they got more lbws and bowlers than any other side that season. It was a simple idea but very effective. Too often we would all talk about hitting back-of-a-length, but then your bowleds and lbws are out of the game. You set a straight field – with mid-on, mid-off, extra cover and mid-wicket – so if they hit fuller deliveries, you have protection. It would depend on the wickets as to how long you classified the ball as being new. Some were abrasive, some weren't.

We went round the table, and I think I said something about getting our batsmen to ensure they stand up more and be in the best possible position to play a short or full ball. That was something we worked hard on at Northern Districts. Domestic cricket in New Zealand was competitive, but at the end of the day the players got on better and were more cordial after play than in county cricket. Both teams talked together about cricket. When I played for Warwickshire Andy Lloyd told us that we had to go and have a drink with the members, only for half an hour, but all of us had to go. The Kiwis just seemed a closer and a friendlier bunch than in county cricket and easier in each other's company. Just as the coaches were all one, so the players were all one at the end of the day for the good of New Zealand cricket – but no less competitive on the field.

A young player who I like to think I helped bring on was a 17-year old Kane Williamson. He was keen to copy the techniques of the best Australians, but his own was so good that he did not need to. From early on, he was so easy to work with. He absorbed everything I told him, while sometimes challenging my reasoning and always asking questions. He never shirked away from hard work and was so single-minded. I worked with him extensively in the off-season after my first season with Northern Districts and gave him his first-class debut in my second, against Otago at Dunedin. I batted him at number three which surprised some good observers such as O'Donnell, but he showed great mental strength and was up to the challenge. Kane's parents wanted him to go to Auckland University, but I explained to them their son was a special talent and would be away touring with New Zealand A and then the main team. I was right. He was picked for both in rapid succession not long after his debut and has never looked back.

My second year as Northern Districts coach was not quite as successful as the first, although we did reach the Twenty20 state final where we lost to Central Districts. We couldn't replicate our four-day form of the previous season, winning just one game in eight. Andrew Strauss spent two months, January and February of 2008, playing for Northern Districts ahead of England's tour of New Zealand in March of that year. He was a very good man to work with, and he helped the youngsters, particularly BJ Watling, with his batting, and Marshall with the captaincy every now and then. He was a great overseas pro. He was a bit like Jimmy Adams at Free State. They both brought with them more than just their batting – above all, their cricketing brain and their prowess. As Strauss had come over with his wife, I thought the honourable thing to do was move out of my rented house in Hamilton and let them have it. I stayed in a local hotel for the two months he was with Northern Districts. It wouldn't have been much fun for him and his wife to live in a hotel for that length of time, but for me on my own it was no problem. When his time with us was over, he joined the England tour of New Zealand and scored a career-best 177 in the third and deciding Test to help England clinch the series 2-1.

Later in 2008 New Zealand toured England where they lost the Test series 2-0, although they did win the one-day series 3-1. In July news leaked that the New Zealand coach, John Bracewell, would be rejoining Gloucestershire in time for the 2009 season. His contract with NZ Cricket ran till then, but people had become fed up with him. There was a strong anti-Bracewell feeling among senior players, who had strong egos and wanted more control of, and influence on, the way they were playing and practising. But Bracewell didn't give them any say, and he led them strongly. In the second half of 2008 NZ Cricket advertised his position, notwithstanding the fact his contract was coming to an end. I think they said he could reapply, but he got the hump, saying if they didn't want him they should sack him.

I applied and was invited for interview in Christchurch. Nobody knows this but, on the day of the interview, I misread the departure time of the flight NZ Cricket had booked for me from Hamilton to Christchurch for my 2pm interview. I arrived at the airport an hour after my 0730 flight and was aghast at my error. There wasn't another flight that day that would have got me to Christchurch on time, and I wondered what on earth to do. So I drove to Auckland an hour away and just made the mid-morning flight to Christchurch, paying for it myself. I arrived there in a sweat, running madly for the taxi rank. Luckily I got to the office 15 mins before my interview, went to the gents toilet and tried to wash myself and get my collar and tie sorted. I needed to get my heartbeat down as this was my big opportunity.

I did not, of course, tell the interviewing panel of my mad dash – how could I? I hadn't even read an email correctly to get the right flight, yet I was applying for the top coaching job in New Zealand. It was the only flight I've ever missed. Luckily the panel didn't notice anything untoward as they were concentrating on their list of candidates. The interview went very well. I told the panel: "Let's be honest, there'll be tears before laughter. If you give it to me, I'll get the guys up, but the seniors need to understand what I want them to do. We'll get there but you'll have to trust me." I was very open with them. I said I desperately wanted the position as it was my dream job, but they would have to show patience as turning the side round would not happen overnight.

Matthew Mott, the Australian who later got the England one-day coaching role, was the front-runner, and I heard that Brendon McCullum favoured him. Mott was apparently offered the job, but he wasn't sure how much he really wanted it and played for time. NZ Cricket finally lost patience after four or five days and issued a take-it-or-leave-it ultimatum. He continued to procrastinate, so they withdrew the offer. Anyway, I was at Hamilton on the ground on an open day doing some practice when I got the call from the CEO of NZ Cricket, Justin Vaughan, who said they wanted to offer me the job as Black Caps coach. I went giddy straightaway with an unbelievable feeling of elation but composed myself. "Great, thanks very much," I stammered. Vaughan continued: "We need you to drive to NZTV offices in Auckland tomorrow morning for a 10am press conference when you'll be on live TV. We haven't got a lot of money, Andy, so we can't pay what England, Australia or India pay but we can offer you $100,000 per annum," That was twice what I was earning at Northern Districts, and I replied: "I'm not in it for the money. Just pay me the market rate here and I'm delighted." "That's what we want to hear," Vaughan declared.

Financially it was a good deal for me as during the eleven months I worked for them, I hardly spent a penny of my salary, as I got 50 NZ dollars a day meal money (about £25). In my time as coach I slept barely a dozen nights in my bed in Hamilton as I was either away touring, travelling around NZ or in South Africa or watching how John Buchanan worked with Calcutta Knight Riders at the IPL. NZ Cricket paid all my expenses for that gig and provided a company car which barely got used. It didn't finish as I would have wanted it to, but when I took the position I knew it was a poisoned chalice because of the strong characters that were in the team: the likes of Brendon McCullum, Kyle Mills, Jacob Oram and Dan Vettori.

Vaughan said not to tell anyone as they hadn't informed Bracewell yet that he had been axed. It was no problem as far as Northern Districts were concerned as NZ Cricket paid the salaries of all the provincial coaches. The New Zealand team were in Australia at the time playing a two-Test series, having just lost the first in Adelaide. For some reason Bracewell heard the news from media reports and was understandably very angry. A week later after losing the second Test in Brisbane by an innings, the team returned to New Zealand and were given five or six days at home before convening again in Dunedin for the first of two Tests against West Indies. I met the team there for the first time, having been told by the selectors we would include three debutants: Tim MacIntosh, James Baker and Dion Nash. Two changes in the batting order I made paid dividends. Daniel Flynn, who had batted at six in Australia, I moved up to number three in place of Jesse Ryder, who I felt was better suited to a spot lower down the order at number five. Gratifyingly Flynn made 95 and Ryder 89 in our total of 365. We reduced West Indies to 173 for six before fast bowler Jerome Taylor rescued them with a maiden first-class hundred off just 97 balls. They were all out for 340, but with both the second and fifth days washed out, a draw was inevitable.

The second Test at Napier was also a high-scoring draw, although we had an outside chance of victory on the final day when we needed 312 from 60 overs. Soon after McCullum was fifth out at 203, Vettori and I called off the chase with 92 still required off nine overs. McCullum was very angry with our decision as he said we never got that many opportunities to win games. Vettori and I thought we had more chance of losing it than winning it, and, looking back, maybe we should have thrown caution to the wind. There were heated arguments with McCullum in the dugout by the side of the pitch. There was always a bit of a battle between Vettori and McCullum as Brendon wanted to be captain. Daniel was a good captain but certainly wasn't a Bazball-type leader.

After the series Vettori told me he wanted more say in the team than he had under Bracewell. I said that was fine by me, but a few weeks later after the T20 and one-day series the CEO Vaughan rang me to say he needed to see me. We met up, and he told me Vettori wanted yet more say in the team. I asked him what he meant. "More hands on," came back the reply. I responded that I believed the captain should be in charge of the team anyway. Vaughan countered: "But he wants to be more involved, so can you just stand back a little bit more." I replied, "If that's what you really want me to do, I'll stand back and let him," although my alarm bells were ringing a little bit. This hadn't happened under Bracewell as he'd ruled them with a rod of iron. I had wanted to create an atmosphere where they felt comfortable, which I think I did, but I suspect I gave away too much ground, which made them think that they could take more. For example, how we practised and when, possibly for shorter periods, but also they just wanted more input in the general running of the team affairs as a group. I wasn't wary of them as such but they had very strong egos, and they assumed control of various matters. After about six months I felt they were extracting more and more.

That second Test finished on December 23, and after a very short Christmas break we met the West Indies in a T20 day-nighter on Boxing Day at Auckland. This was only the second time we had played against West Indies in this format, the first having also been at Auckland three years earlier. That had ended in a tie, with a bowl-out going in New

Zealand's favour, and by the strangest quirk the second meeting on the same ground also ended in a tie. The difference was that this time there was a 'super' over to decide the outcome. As Vettori had bowled superbly to return 4-0-16-3 in the main event, he was entrusted with it. Sadly for us, it cost 25 after Chris Gayle hit him for three sixes. We only received four balls back as we lost two wickets and were well beaten. A chastened Vettori did not care for the concept of a super over, complaining to the media that "the game's called Twenty20, not One1." Gayle mischievously described it as "the best one-over match I've ever played."

I had persuaded NZ Cricket to hire Dermot Reeve, who was out in New Zealand, as an advisor for the T20 and one-day international series against West Indies. He had been a brilliant one-day captain at Warwickshire, and I thought his input could be invaluable. That night back at the hotel after the super over, however, he, McCullum, Ross Taylor and I were having a drink at the bar. I went to bed, but Dermot stayed up and, as I heard from McCullum the next morning, proceeded to tell him and Taylor that he, Reeve, was much better qualified to coach New Zealand than I was. As I'd gone to the trouble of bringing him on board, I felt betrayed but said nothing to him about it. We were driving down in a couple of team minibuses that morning from Auckland to Hamilton, where the second T20 was due to be played the next day, but had to stop half-way to allow Reeve to get off the bus and be sick by the side of the road. Evidently he had had a drink or two too many the previous night. Dermot stayed on with the team for another fortnight, but that was the end of his involvement. I never told him about McCullum's revelation to me.

In the first T20 McCullum, opening, had got out early on, dancing down the wicket trying to hit inside out over extra for six. We'd got an inexperienced batting lineup and only made 155 at Auckland, and I was keen for him to try to bat longer to lay the basis for a bigger total in Hamilton. So I said to him when we went out at Seddon Park to have a look at the wicket, "Baz, can you give me seven or eight overs of you just batting so that we can get these young kids into the game and settle the team? Pull back on the reins, get into the game and then go." He replied: "No, Moler, I'm busy building brand McCullum." "Pardon?

The team needs you," I pleaded. "No, no, sorry about what the team needs. I'm building a brand, and it's called Brand McCullum. This is how I play." I found that very difficult – that he didn't do what I wanted him to do for the team. The next day McCullum proceeded to smash 59 in an opening stand of 130 off just 70 balls with Jesse Ryder as we posted 191 in our 20 overs. That was too much for the West Indies. Brand McCullum was up and running. And everywhere he's gone, he's got his own brand of cricket – over-aggressive as a batsman, over-aggressive as a coach. Who says he's wrong? Look at him now. Bazball is Brand McCullum. He's been a very successful player, and he's changed the way a lot of batters play.

I got on with him OK, but he had wanted Mott as coach, not me, and there were little things between us. I remember feeding the bowling machine to him at the ICC World Twenty20 in England at the Oval in 2009. We were off for rain against Scotland. He smacked a couple of balls that he could have hit anywhere straight back like tracer bullets a couple of metres to my left. I was thinking "Is he aiming at me?" but instead I shouted, "Hey, great shot." Then he crunched one and it hit the bowling machine right in front of my face. I looked at him and asked "why, why?" He retorted "I'm just practising," but I thought "No, I'm not so sure, mate." His elder brother, Nathan, an off-spinner who batted a bit, was a totally different character, a lovely mellow chap who I got on fantastically well with. I got on well enough with Brendon, but there was just something there. The best players always have that little bit of something in them. And Brendon McCullum has got that bit of mongrel in him. I respect him highly as a cricketer, but sometimes you have to think about other people.

There were times when his 'Brand McCullum' took over, but who's to say he was wrong? He's changed the attitude of New Zealand cricket. He's led from the front as a captain. He got some runs when I was coach – not loads – as an opener in one-dayers and at number six in Tests before he gave up the gloves. He was a very good keeper; he used a brand new pair of gloves for every Test as he said the pimples had to be fresh. He'd wear a new pair and break in another pair during that Test for the next Test by pumping his bat handle into the middle of the glove to make an indentation. He was just a difficult person to manage.

I thought he could have been more of a team man at times, but kudos to him. He was building his brand, which he's done very well.

Other players needed treating differently. Kyle Mills, who topped the ICC's ODI bowling rankings in 2009, was quite injury-prone and was always complaining about something – he was a moaner. Jacob Oram was a lovely guy but soft. I'd heard he was often injured and complained he was always having to play when only 80% fit. So the first time I met him, I said, "Go away and do not come back till you're 100% fit." He really appreciated that, and I always got on well with him. Jesse Ryder was one helluva character and probably the most talented cricketer I ever worked with. He could amble up and bowl at 140 clicks, was a great slip catcher and a brilliant backward point, and would turn the game around as a batsman. But he had no discipline from a troubled childhood. We found out he had an alcohol problem – when he had one drink, he had to have 101. It annoyed the senior players that we said that if he went out, another player had to go with him and keep an eye on him. Their view was that he should be able to look after himself. But the CEO Vaughan said the medical staff were adamant that we had to look after him.

After the third one-day international against West Indies in Wellington, which we'd won by seven wickets, he told us he was going out to celebrate with some of his mates. The next morning, we were due to leave at 8.30am on the team bus for the airport. At 8.25 he arrived back at the hotel absolutely bladdered, with two drunken mates helping him through the door. "Hello, coach," he slurred. I told him to go to bed and that we were leaving without him. For disciplinary reasons we left him out of the fourth one-dayer two days later in Auckland, where his replacement, Martin Gupthill, became the first player of any nationality for 13 years to score a hundred on debut in ODIs.

Ryder didn't drink every day, once going 40 days without a drink he told me, but there were a number of alcohol-induced infractions involving him. It was a great shame as he had so much natural ability. That same New Zealand summer, he batted brilliantly against India, scoring a maiden one-day international hundred off just 72 balls in Christchurch, and then, ten days later, a maiden Test century in Hamilton. In the next Test in Napier, he trumped that with 201, helping New Zealand to pass 600 for only the third time in their history. India followed on, but Gautham Gambier then batted ten hours and 43 minutes for his 137 to deny us victory. He scored another hundred in the third Test, which was also a draw, giving India a 1-0 series win, their first on New Zealand soil for 41 years.

If it was a disappointment as coach not to have presided over a win in five home Tests that New Zealand summer – the two against West Indies having been drawn – it was a privilege to watch Sachin Tendulkar bat at close quarters. It transpired that Hamilton, the venue for the first Test, was one of the few grounds where he'd never scored a hundred. The day before the match, he got his son to feed the bowling machine, which was behind the cricket offices at Hamilton. When you were in them, you could hear this 'boom, boom' every time a ball hit the bat. For an hour or hour and half Tendulkar defended or left balls, not playing one attacking shot. I watched a fair bit of it, but some of our people there heard him say he was going to block a hundred as he wanted one at Hamilton so much. And when he scored one in India's first innings, it was one of the most painful pleasures I witnessed. After being dropped on 13 he did block his way to a hundred, playing straight without any extravagant shots, with every ball treated on its merits. He just completed the job, and the discipline in his play was pure magic to watch. Thanks to his 160, India amassed 520, the platform for a ten-wicket win.

Gary Kirsten was coaching the Indians. I agreed with him that, in the two days before each Test, we'd have the morning at the ground for practice and they'd have the afternoon. The next day it was the other way round. He managed them very well as the Indians didn't like to practise like the Kiwis or South Africans, who preferred a busy practice with cones, warming up, stretching and then bowling in the middle. The Indians, though, had just four or five in a semi-circle for catches, that was their warm-up. They just did what they wanted to do, and Gary recognised that, saying "OK, whilst you're winning, we'll do it your way." On more than one occasion he messaged me to say we could have the ground all day as they were not coming to practice. They won the both Test and ODI series, and we took the T20 series 2-0.

Four months later, we toured Sri Lanka for a two-Test series, a pair of T20s and a triangular 50-over tournament with India that was preparation for the ICC Champions Trophy in South Africa. We had a pretty inexperienced squad and it showed in the Tests, both of which we lost on turning pitches. We struggled, like so many visiting teams there, to counter Mutthiah Muralitharan who claimed 13 wickets in the two Tests. Vettori picked up ten himself, as well as scoring a hundred from number eight in the second Test. In doing so, he became only the second New Zealander, after Richard Hadlee, to claim 300 Test wickets. Tim Southee, to whom I had given a first-class debut as a teenager when I was Northern Districts coach, has since become the third.

We did, however, win both T20s to continue our good form in the format after beating India at home. I got an email from the CEO, saying well done on the T20s and that the board wanted to add me to the selection committee. This would now consist of the captain, me, Glenn Turner, John Wright and another board member. Previously I'd sat in on them and answered questions but didn't get a vote. After a couple of 50-over matches in Sri Lanka that we lost, we flew straight to South Africa for the ICC Champions Trophy. When South Africa beat us in our opening group game to make it six defeats in our last seven games, expectations were not high but we won our two other group games against Sri Lanka and England to reach the semi-finals. Frustratingly Jesse Ryder, who hammered 74 from 58 balls against Sri Lanka, pulled a groin muscle in the process and had to withdraw from the tournament. So too, with a hand injury, did Daryl Tuffey after that game, with Jacob Oram also sent home early with a back problem. We felt the loss of this trio later in the tournament.

England had already qualified for the semis when we met them as they had already beaten both Sri Lanka and South Africa. I don't think there was any complacency on their part though, although they misjudged the conditions, being over-aggressive on a pitch with uneven bounce. Vettori showed magnanimous sportsmanship when he recalled Paul Collingwood when he casually left his crease before making his ground at the end of an over and was run out by McCullum, who threw down the stumps. The irony was not lost on us as Collingwood had refused to recall Grant Elliott a year earlier at the Oval when he collided with Ryan Sidebottom while trying to take a run. Vettori told the media that "the spirit of cricket is at the forefront of everyone's mind at the moment." It was probably poetic justice when Elliott took four for 31 to help skittle England for 146, which we knocked off with nearly 23 overs to spare. Beating England was bitter-sweet with all my mates in England getting hold of me, saying well done. It had been quite strange standing up to two national anthems before the game.

Elliott also starred with the bat in our semi-final win over Pakistan at the Wanderers, making an unbeaten 75 to help chase down a target of 234. Pakistan had got through to the last four thanks to beating India comfortably, both sides having overcome a weak West Indies. As all the teams were staying in the same Joburg hotel, word got out about an unfortunate off-field scandal that may have put India off their stride. An embarrassing dossier attributed to Gary Kirsten, their coach, was made public, encouraging sex for their players to increase testosterone levels and, with it, more aggression on the field. The devoutly religious Kirsten eventually issued a statement revealing that Paddy Upton, the Indian team's mental-conditioning expert, was the author of the dossier.

Australia were our opponents in the final after they thrashed England in the other semi at Centurion where the final was to be played. England had made the mistake of batting first there in what was a day-nighter, which I knew from years of playing and coaching in South Africa was a bad idea because of dew in early October on the highveld. That made it difficult for spinners in particular to grip the ball. Unfortunately, Vettori injured a hamstring after slipping in the morning of the final, ruling him out of it. My assistant coach, Mark O'Donnell, and I were concerned that McCullum, who took over the captaincy, would bat first, and said to him. "Baz, we've got to chase if we win the toss. We know South African conditions, we've both coached here, we've looked at the stats. You've got to chase." He replied: "No, no, we're gonna bat first." I said: "Captain, listen to both of us, we're giving you the benefit of our experience of being in this country. You might have played here once or twice; we've both coached here for five years. We know conditions here. Teams batting second here win more often than not." "No, no, we're gonna bat first," he insisted.

We duly batted first after winning the toss, and McCullum, opening, got a duck, facing 12 balls in the process. We made only 200. Australia knocked the runs off, with Jeetan Patel, Vettori's replacement, conceding 44 off 6.2 overs as he was unable to grip a wet ball. If Daniel had played, and we'd fielded first, we'd have had a great chance as the Centurion pitch turned. The Aussie off-spinner Nathan Hauritz took three for 37 from his ten overs, including two top-order wickets. So I left there very disappointed, but consoling myself we'd got to a final. It wasn't very often New Zealand got to finals at that stage.

Before we went to Sri Lanka, our new team manager, Dave Currie, who had been the chef de mission of New Zealand's Olympic and Commonwealth Games teams, had gone to the board to ask for more say. He told me I was too soft on the players. I suggested he should let me decide about that and that he should concentrate on admin. "No, I've spoken to the rowing coaches in the Olympic team," he replied, "and they said they can get their rowers to row within a tenth of a second of their personal bests every time." I didn't see the connection with cricket and questioned: "Really, is it always the same the water? Is it choppy? If the wind blows too much, they cancel the racing, don't they? They only race four times a year. We have to go on tour where we play multiple days. No rower would row close to his personal best if they had to do that."

Currie retorted with the absurd recommendation that what the players should be doing between Test matches was running half-marathons. I laughed it off, again asking him to concentrate on flights, hotels and logistics and let me and the captain worry about the cricketing side of things. But he got into the ear of NZ Cricket, arguing the manager of the All Blacks had more say than the coach. He certainly wanted more say and was another who was chipping away at my post. He'd had no experience of playing, and the players hated him. Jesse Ryder, for one, twice gave him what the Aussies call a 'verbal spray' – a piece of his mind.

If any player had a birthday, Currie would exclaim at the start of the day, "All together now, happy birthday dear so-and-so, happy birthday to you, happy birthday dear so-and-so, happy birthday to you." He also urged the players to perform the haka before every Test match, just like the All Blacks. They looked at him suspiciously and clearly didn't think it was a good idea. I told him that the haka was not our thing, but that if the Maori players wanted to do it they could bring the idea into the team environment. Needless to say, they didn't. He just was not well-liked and eventually left a few months after I was sacked. He had been recruited by the CEO, with whom he had a very good relationship, as well as being supported by Geoff Allott, the new director of cricket, who wanted all management to be New Zealanders.

After the final I went from Pretoria to Bloemfontein to see my family for a two-week break that had been agreed beforehand. But 24 hours later, I got a phone call from Currie, saying I need to get on a plane back to NZ straightaway and have a meeting with the board in Christchurch. "There are serious issues you have to face," he said. "What do you mean? What are you talking about?" I asked. "We'll let you know when you get here," he replied. "We've booked your flight for tomorrow morning."

I was left wondering what on earth was going on. I tried to ring Vettori, but he didn't answer his phone. Nor did some other senior players I called. Nevertheless, I aborted my leave and caught the flight to New Zealand as directed. I got back and saw the CEO Vaughan, who declared things were not working with me as coach. I asked that he let me talk to the players, and that if they didn't want me I'd leave. However, I'd just got the team to a world final, and I'd given Daniel more rope that he wanted. Our stats were quite good; we could have done better but we were improving. So I didn't understand where this was coming from.

Vaughan continued: "The players don't want you. It's not you're a bad coach. You're not the type of coach they want." I responded indignantly: "You employed me. Why don't you back me?" "Well, we've got to listen to the players," he replied. I had still been ringing the players but none were answering, so they obviously knew what was going on.

Nevertheless, the board arranged for me and Dan to have a chat at the hotel bar in Christchurch with Geoff Allott. The conversation went something like this. "Well, Moler, you don't do that much coaching now, you just manage the coaches," Vettori said. "Well, I was told to give you more say and let you have what you want. Are you telling me you can't work with me?" I replied. "No, I'm not saying I can't work with you," he admitted. "So what do you want me to change? I'm enjoying the job. What do you want?" I asked. But he didn't answer the question and was very wishy-washy.

We had hit a brick wall, and I realised my time was up, which was a bitter disappointment. I had been in the post for under a year and had been sacked days after taking us to a world final no one had expected us to reach. One we might have won had Brendon McCullum not gone against advice and fielded first instead of second with a wet ball. I was devastated and rejected NZ Cricket's pitiful offer of three months' severance pay when I had seven months left on my contract. We didn't get much further before Vaughan announced that NZ Cricket would go to arbitration as he thought it was an unresolvable situation.

I rang Tim Munton in England to get his thoughts as he has always had a wise head on him. It proved a propitious call as he revealed that when he played for Wellington for a winter in his early days as a young professional, one of his team-mates ended up becoming a leading lawyer in New Zealand. Tim gave me his name, Mark Freeman, and told me to give him a call. When I did so, he passed me on to one of his colleagues, Rob Towner, a top Human Resources lawyer. When I spoke to him, he replied that he'd read about my issues in the papers and that NZ Cricket's behaviour was not on. I explained how they'd backed me into a corner, and I didn't know what to do about it. He said not to worry and that he'd see me in Auckland the next morning at 9am.

He sat me down in his office, listened to the whole story, taking detailed notes, and then asked if I'd had any reviews. I replied that all I'd had was one phone call in Sri Lanka from Geoff Allott when I was added to the selection committee and was told I was doing a good job. "Any paper trail?" he asked. "None," I replied, which he said was good.

The arbitration hearing had been set for 48 hours later, but before it there was the end-of-season awards dinner, which was televised and a big event in New Zealand. He said, "You must go to that tomorrow night. It's going to be uncomfortable as all the players have been trying to get rid of you, but you sit there and you smile." When I turned up at the awards dinner, the players were flabbergasted as they thought

I'd gone. I said, 'Hello guys, how you going? Looking forward to the Bangladesh tour?" New Zealand were off there ten days or so later.

It had been in the papers that NZ Cricket were taking me to arbitration. I was on the their table, just general chatting to a board member from Auckland, while I could sense the players were looking at me. It was very, very uncomfortable. The board member said to me, "Andy, I'm sorry to hear what's happening, but it is what it is." I replied, "Yes, but let's see what happens." He asked if I'd got a lawyer and I said I had. He asked who it was. When I told him Rob Towner, he smiled, "You'll be fine then. Just follow his word to the letter. NZ Cricket don't know what's going to hit them."

The next morning I got up for breakfast and came down in the hotel lift to the ground floor. As it opened, standing right in front of me was Vettori, who'd blanked me the night before. He acknowledged me this time. "All right, captain?" I asked him. He looked me in the eye and replied: "Andy, you're going to hear some things that aren't going be very nice but just get the best deal that you can, please. I like you and thank you for everything." The irony was not lost on me, for it was him who'd instigated the moves to get rid of me.

I went straight to the arbitration hearing in Auckland, where my lawyer Rob Towner was waiting for me. "Leave it with me, I've got all my notes ready," he assured me. After we'd moved into in the hearing room, in walked the arbitrator, who shook my hand. He confided, "I know your lawyer, and we've done lots of cases together. You're in very good hands. I've read what's in the papers and, if the reports are true, you're going to do very well today."

Then in walked the NZ Cricket CEO, Justin Vaughan, with their lawyer. My lawyer then proceeded to destroy NZ Cricket's case. "Where's your paper trail that you say he's incompetent?" he began. "When have you had any conversations about it with him? Why did you say he was doing a good job when you brought him onto the selection panel? What's the HR policy of NZ cricket? He's got diabetes that's been out of control since you started this whole thing; his personal and mental health has been affected." Their lawyer just sat there and took it and took it. My lawyer was just unbelievable, and he said to the arbitrator, "Sir, I think we're done on this side of the table. Is there anything they want to say." They just said, "No, nothing."

The arbitrator said, "Right we're going to go to different rooms now, and New Zealand Cricket I hope you've brought your cheque book." He got me my full contract paid out plus money for mental distress; he hit them hard. NZC also had to pay my lawyers' costs as well. When I told the arbitrator I'd be leaving in ten days' time for South Africa, as I had ends to tie up, he ordered NZC not to take my mobile phone back they had got for me until I was at the airport about to leave the country.

While the results of the hearing were a total vindication on my part, I was very sad to leave a country I had grown extremely fond of after three very fulfilling years there. I now felt very disillusioned with the game I had always loved. And I took no pleasure from New Zealand's disastrous collapse in form under my temporary replacement as coach, Mark Greatbatch, on their tour of Bangladesh and India straight after. They lost a one-day series in Bangladesh 4-0, "playing like dicks" as Greatbatch complained publicly. They then went to India where they lost a three-match Test series 1-0 before being hammered 5-0 in the one-day series.

The reality behind my dismissal was that players wanted hands-on control of the team – total control. Vettori was also the coach with Greatbatch in Bangladesh and India. I had liked Dan but he wanted total control so that if it all went wrong, it was down to him. I did lose respect for him at the end when it became apparent he wasn't being upfront with me. He was a good leader and thinker on the game. He thought that was the best thing for the team. I don't think he's a vindictive person. He's a driven person who wanted to change things around and to do it his way, not somebody else's way. Behind that, you had McCullum, who wanted to captain the team as well as do things his way as well. There was always a banging of heads between them; you also had Kyle Mills who swung one way and the other between the pair, but closer to McCullum; Jacob Oram would amble along and was a carefree spirit basically. Then there was Geoff Allott, who wanted a Kiwi coach. He fought with me as I had Mark O'Donnell, and Allott wanted a different coach for every series so that players got different ideas.

Mark rang me recently from his native New Zealand, where he has had a successful coaching career since, and confirmed how New Zealand's cricketers of that time prided themselves about not back-stabbing fellow players or coaches: "That is quite correct, Moler," he said. "The saying was 'in the belly not the back'. On the next tour after you had left, I had to go as assistant coach. I went to the first net practice and didn't say anything to the players other than what I had to from a coaching point of view. After it, Vettori said we needed to have a chat back at the hotel.

"I agreed that we did, and once there, he asked, 'Are we OK?' I replied: 'How you did that with Andy Moles was f***ing disgraceful.' He said: 'Yes, you are right, but I wasn't allowed to say anything to Andy or you. Dave Currie told me not to. And the legal advice was not to say anything as it's going to litigation.' I told Dan that was f***ing rubbish, and that how it was handled was a disgrace. If we had won that ICC trophy, I don't think they could have got rid of you, Moler. You could see the water trail from the dew when Jeetan Patel came on to bowl under the lights. I can still remember McCullum coming up to me in the hotel after the match and asking if I was still pissed off with him for batting first. I told him in no uncertain terms I was."

All hell broke out with the press after my sacking. They wanted to get me on talk-shows. I said, "No, no, it's over now, that's it. I've got nothing to say. That's it. I don't want to talk about it." I was very bitter. I fell out of love with the game. I came back to Cape Town and later worked for the University of the Western Cape. My love for the game only developed again when I became their coach. The way NZ Cricket treated me, the way these players made me feel, I felt like a second-class citizen. I hadn't played Test cricket, and I think they wanted a Test coach.

Greatbatch took over in the interim, but he only lasted the one tour, although he wanted it to be longer. He'd been sacked by Warwickshire. John Wright, who was Greatbatch's successor, was a lovely man. Some players are so fickle, for when I was New Zealand coach, I'd wanted Wright to come and talk to us in Hamilton about his experiences as a Test batsman. McCullum came out and said, "We don't want him here, he's geriatric. We don't want him anywhere near us. We want new fresh ideas, not what he's got." Then six months later, Wright was their coach. I don't know how he did, because by then I didn't care about New Zealand cricket because of the way I was treated. They'd taken the love of the game away from me, those egotistical buggers. They made me question why on earth I was involved with cricket. I was away from my family, and for a time I hated the game. That's how they made me feel. It did hit my mental health, getting me to fly back 24 hours after the ICC Champions Trophy when I'd been promised two weeks' leave, having been away from home for six months and not seen my kids in that time.

Currie, the team manager, drove it. He fed the fire with the players, and he knew he'd get the responses he wanted. Suddenly they had too much player power after having had none under John Bracewell. Maybe I should have used a stick. But I trusted Vettori. I've seen him briefly once since, but when I did the walk for charity after my leg was cut off he sent a $500 donation. Mark's voicemail confirms he knew that he didn't cover himself in glory. If I saw him today, I'd shake his hand and give him a man-hug and say, "Lovely to see you. It's gone now. It's over." But at the time I just couldn't believe he'd gone away from the team motto, 'In the belly not in the back'. They lived by that, but they didn't live by that with me. My last big international game was a world final. How many coaches get sacked after being in a world final? New Zealand had only been in one once before in their history. It was the players who had got us to the final – and good on them – but you had to think I had some influence on the environment.

Tribute
by Andrew Strauss
England cricketer

I first heard of Andy as a young guy in my teens looking through the scorecards every morning when I saw he was part of that very strong Warwickshire side of the mid-90s. So I was really interested to meet him when I went to Northern Districts for a couple of months. What I saw was a guy who was a great people person, who loved interacting with people and was incredibly passionate about the game of cricket, and batting in particular. I think he showed the qualities that all really good coaches have, which is not so much about technique or game awareness but about people. It's about understanding what makes people tick and then building a trusting relationship with people. That's what he was really good at. He was a very kind, sensitive person, who could be emotional at times. He cared passionately about the club at Northern Districts, the job he was doing and about the team he was coaching.

At that stage, I was going through a bit of a mental crisis as I'd been dropped by the England cricket team for the first time in my life. I went to Northern Districts, probably erroneously on reflection, to play T20 and a bit of 50-over cricket. I was battling with myself at that stage. What I really benefited from were the long discussions off the field in the evenings with Andy, generally around life and more philosophical stuff. That is, in a lot of ways, more powerful than anything. What I was working my way through mentally at the stage was this idea of letting go a bit, almost not trying too hard, accepting that there's only so much you can control and giving myself a break mentally. Going to Northern Districts was useful in that respect because it's a quiet place, Hamilton, in the middle of nowhere. You had a lot of time on your own. It was a long way away from the hustle and bustle of cricket at elite level. So you tap back into why you play the game in the first place, and Andy helped remind me.

I stayed with Andy a bit before my wife Ruth came to New Zealand, but when she did he moved out to a hotel to give us some privacy. That was the measure of the man: his dedication to the cause and his selflessness. I sensed he was very much married to the game of cricket and that was his great love really. With that came a lot of satisfaction but also a degree of anxiety and pressure because we all know that cricket can be a very fickle mistress.

Tribute

by Kane Williamson

New Zealand cricketer

I have nothing but positive memories of Andy when he was coach at Northern Districts, where he is fondly remembered. The side was very unified under him. There was no split between the back and the front of the team bus. He really helped me mentally and technically as a 16/17-year-old trying to make my way in the professional game, as in that time teams were more hard-nosed towards young aspiring players. He was especially good with young cricketers, passing on the wisdom and experiences that he had gained from his own playing career. I really am grateful to him for the assistance he gave me at the start of my career. I didn't break into the New Zealand side until after he'd left as national coach, but I consider him to be a very important early influence on my career. He will always have my respect and empathy.

15

Reviving my love for the game

I arrived back home in South Africa severely bruised at my sudden departure from New Zealand. Now I was out of work, so I got onto an agent called Arthur Turner, who was CEO at Griquas when I played there. He'd set up a sports agency in Cape Town, and we met for a coffee when I asked him if there was anything around and to keep me in mind. Six months or so later, in the South African winter of 2010, he contacted me and said there could be an interesting coaching challenge at the University of the Western Cape, an institution with predominantly coloured and black students. It had been established really for people from the disadvantaged community, the intake being 85-90% coloured or black. They had a cricket NGO called Sports Skills for Life Skills, supported by the De Villiers Graaf family, who are massive landowners in the western Cape. They put in a couple of million rand a year to uplift the coloured community. It was a wonderful project that is still going after 15 years. They were looking for a coach for the cricket side for the 2010/11 season. They couldn't pay me much, but it was enough for my living expenses.

My now partner, Megan, had moved to Cape Town, so I had come there with her. I ended up working full-time at the university for two seasons. We had up to three practice sessions per week in the afternoon and evenings, but in term-time only. As all the students went home during the holiday periods, we caught up on our fixtures in term-time by playing on a Sunday with two games a weekend instead of one. The lads for my first year were a really good mix of second and third year students and 19-year old school-leavers. I have a talent for challenging young players to reach their potential, but to do that, it requires hard work – no shortcuts with an emphasis on physical fitness, mental preparation and skills preparation. I quickly made a link with this group of players, of which three or four were really good ones who played the odd second team game for Western Province Cobras. The whole group straightaway bought into my ethos of hard work and supporting each other. Northern Districts professionally were the closest to the dressing-room environment we had at Warwickshire, but these guys came very close to being exactly the same as that. The first, second and third teams all ended up winning their respective leagues in my first season as coach. To win the Western Province first division, which included all the best Cape Town clubs, was an outstanding achievement for a team comprised mainly of coloureds, with a sprinkling of whites and blacks.

The university and its grounds were in an industrial coloured area, but we enjoyed excellent facilities. The wickets were quite dry, and we had two very good spinners. We always tried to bat first and then knock the opposition over. One of them went on to play for Western Province – Emanuel Sererami – who passed his law degree and is now in charge of Eastern Province ladies' cricket. The players listened and enjoyed the training. We had a physio who joined us from the physio department of the uni at every practice and all our games (paid for by the NGO) as well as a fitness trainer, who was doing the sports science degree. The second and third teams each had a physio, fitness trainer and coach. The other clubs didn't have anything like that, so the whole club was run like a professional organisation.

I got my love of cricket back through them, thanks to the way they bought into me unquestionably. I enjoyed the atmosphere in the dressing-room where their camaraderie was excellent. They supported each other and enjoyed each other's success. This environment we created was just fantastic to be involved in; it had everything we had at Warwickshire and Northern Districts. It was what retriggered my love of the game. Nic Kock was the guy in charge of the programme, a very liberal white professor who lectured at the uni and was an umpire. We didn't agree on everything; we clashed on certain things such as when his communications with me suddenly stopped after we got relegated in the second year, after five of the best players had graduated at the end of my first year. Kock worked tirelessly, loading up all the meals for the three teams in his 4x4 (all paid for by the charity, supported by De Villiers Graaf with a bit of sponsorship). The charity gave full bursaries for under-privileged students, with fees, accommodation and food all sponsored.

After two seasons at the University of Western Cape, it was time to move on as I wanted to get back into first-class cricket. My agent put my name forward, and in the April of 2012 I became coach for South Western Districts, who were based at Oudtshoorn, some 40 miles northwest of George. It was very very hot there, even hotter than Kimberley. You were looking at around 44^{0}C every day in the cricket season, with hot nights. In winter it was very cold with frosts at night. Unfortunately I walked into another political nightmare as the board, who didn't tell me at the time, had their own restrictions as well as the UCB's quotas to fulfil. Four players had to be black and four coloured. We also had to promote local cricket; eight players had to be home-grown. So your hands were tied behind your back. We had some good players, such as Ottniel Baartman whom I recommended should go on and play better standard than B section first-class cricket. He did and later got picked for South Africa. Another coloured lad, Glenton Stuurman, was the same; he needed better cricket to develop. This angered the board, who wanted to keep the players. Stuurman went on a tour to New Zealand and played a couple of Tests. Andrea Agathangelou, who played for Lancashire and Leicestershire, was a good leader with an excellent work ethic. His target was to hit 500 balls a day – his own rule – and he scored a mountain of runs. We played Boland, Griqualand West, Inland Natal and Eastern Transvaal, home and away, to make it eight four-day games a season and eight one-dayers.

I enjoyed it as it was all about developing young players. They all bought into my philosophy, and camaraderie improved. But apart from Agathangelou, batters averaged in the 20s and never won games for us. The reason they failed was that selection didn't work because of the quota system. You couldn't bring in coloureds from outside the region; they had to be home-grown and born inside South Western Districts (Oudtshoorn and George). You could, however, bring blacks in; we used to get them from Eastern Cape and Border, which is a prime development area for black African cricket. At least we didn't get relegated, finishing lower mid-table. I did two seasons there and enjoyed the challenge of bringing on youngsters, producing those two who went on to play for South Africa. It was a quiet backwater with no social life that consisted of braais, which one or two players came round to. It was time for a new challenge.

16

Afghanistan

Towards the end of 2013 my agent contacted me to say the Afghanistan Cricket Board wanted someone to go there for a week as batting coach. I thought it was an exciting opportunity but then started to wonder what I might have let myself in for. What was happening in Afghanistan was on the news every night. I rang my brother Mark, whose knowledge of anti-terrorism was second to none. When I told him I was going to Kabul, he shot back, "No, you're not." I replied: "Well, I am actually – for five days." "Bloody hell," he retorted. "Right, the first thing I've got to do is list a string of questions because if you get kidnapped, we need proof of life." "What are you on about?" I cut in. "Listen to me, anyone who goes there has to do this," he advised. "The questions will be first, what was the name of our first dog? Squire. Secondly, what village did we live in Lancashire when Dad was posted up there when we were very young? Freckleton. Thirdly, what's Mum's maiden name? Green. And last, where did you meet Jacqui? Kimberley. If you do get taken, at some stage when they start negotiating, this is standard operating procedure and proof of life. They are the four questions you'll be asked as no one will pay any ransom or come and get you if they're not answered correctly."

For this one initial week in Afghanistan I just went on that basis. Later, when I was there 'properly' in the longer term, I had anti-terrorism kidnapping insurance along with medical insurance. The four questions my brother set were lodged with the insurance company, as kidnapping was a major concern in Afghanistan, both by the Taliban and criminal gangs. The way I got there was to fly Emirates from Cape Town to Dubai, then proceed to another terminal and wait there. Then it was another Emirates flight to Kabul. On the way to Dubai on my first trip to Afghanistan, I couldn't but help think why I was doing something this crazy – going to a war-zone, where kidnapping is rife. At Dubai I was now at the gate at the second terminal waiting to board the flight to

Kabul. It was a bit like apartheid: on one side were all the Afghans with their long beards and flowing robes; on the other were all the squaddies and security people who were flying out there. They'd got crew cuts and were big guys with muscles. I got talking to one or two of them and received advice like, "Don't go out at night." So I got on the plane and there was an Afghan male sitting in my seat. I politely informed him he was in my seat but he replied sternly, "No I'm sitting here; you go somewhere else." I asked him to look at his boarding pass but he shook his head. What transpired was that his wife was sitting in the next seat but there was no way he was going to let a white man sit next to her. The stewardess saw what was happening, came down the aisle and politely asked me to follow her to another spare seat as she'd come across this sort of episode before and wanted simply to defuse it. This was the first time I encountered this anti-European feeling from the locals.

On arrival in Kabul we got off the plane and I was met by a local Afghan at Customs, which he'd somehow accessed. On this, my first trip to Kabul, I was classified as a VVIP, a very, very important person, which was why he was at Customs to greet me. He recognised me from a photo, I presumed, and was waving his hands at me. He ushered my luggage through the x-ray machines and hustled me through the arrivals hall to the outside area, where there was an armoured Cherokee limousine waiting for me. It had a guy in the front seat with an AK47 assault rifle and another guy in the back seat with a revolver. We got in the back and departed, but the traffic was awful and so heavy we just crawled along. We eventually got to the hotel in the middle of Kabul, and I was escorted to reception by the guy with the AK47 and checked in.

Ten minutes later we were off again to the cricket ground, which had a brick wall all the way around it. In Kabul they had something called the 'ring of steel', which is a concrete barrier with checkpoints blocking every road that comes into Kabul. There would be twenty to thirty soldiers on each one with sandbags and machine guns. They checked every car and everyone's papers. If I recall correctly, it was about 10km in circumference and started about 5kms from the centre. We reached the ground which was about a kilometre outside this ring of steel in the outskirts but still very populated. The ground had its own security, with big sliding doors and a boom barrier. As we drove in, I could not but notice heavily armed guard towers which were located every 100 metres along this wall. It was a stadium of about 10,000, and it was always packed to the rafters whenever there was any cricket being played. They had to turn people away – they love cricket there. So much so that, once outside the ring of steel on any sort of barren land or clearing, there was a game of cricket going on with kids. There was a park opposite the entrance to the ground which was dust, with not a blade of grass, but on their weekend (Fridays and Saturdays) there would be a dozen or so games of cricket going on, all overlapping and chaotic but it worked somehow. Cricket is a religion for Afghans, just like in India and Pakistan. So I went into the ground and met the CEO and the head coach as well as having a look at the ground. I was there for about an hour, and then it was back to the hotel in the armoured car with the guy with the AK47.

The longer you're in Afghanistan, and the more they get used to you, you become not a VVIP but a VIP, a very important person, as I discovered on subsequent trips when I was contracted. I would still have the armoured car, but no guy with an AK47 and no one to meet me at Customs. Then over time as familiarity began to set in, I became just an IP, an important person. I didn't get an armoured car any more, just a wreck of a car with a driver. To blend in with the locals, I stopped shaving, dressed shabbily, wore a cap or an Afghan hat to try and look like a local. Then I became just 'a person', which meant the car was never there on time and I had to wait around in the airport car park for the driver to come and find me. I'd then be dropped off the other side of the road from the hotel and had to walk across it to get inside the security for the hotel. Then, in the morning, they'd pick me up on the roadside outside the hotel security. You'd be open to kidnap then, and it was often then that the gangs used to seize westerners. Anyway, I'd cross the road and get in the front seat with the driver in this jalopy of a car. I'm talking battered here, a real rustbucket. I used to go to Kabul for a maximum five to six weeks at a time, then come home. When a new chairman of the board came in, I'd go back to being a VVIP for a time as he would want to make sure I was looked after. He was the man in charge, not the CEO. What he said went. But you'd go from being a VVIP to a person in a matter of a week.

At the nets I had one-to-one sessions with five of the top batters for the four days I had in Kabul on my initial visit. They assumed they knew everything, and the problem was that they just wanted to thrash the ball, just hit fours and sixes. They got bored with the concept of building an innings, and that was their downfall. They judged themselves by how many fours and sixes they hit, but I tried to get them to come around to the notion that the more balls they faced, the more fours and six they could hit. You're building partnerships and getting the game further down the line. The crowd in Afghan roared when they hit fours and sixes, but if they didn't, they'd just boo them. Their only currency was fours and sixes, especially sixes. Their fitness was poor, which I addressed later. Playing with the spin, as opposed to playing against the spin, which a lot of them did was the other area I focused on. I tried to help them sweep and to try to get them to hit the sight screen as often as they could – in other words play straight – as they used to play across the line. At the end of my four days I left a report for the CEO, with whom I had got along well.

Back in South Africa, the 2013/14 season was now over, and when I saw an ad by Wellingborough School in Northamptonshire for an ex-professional to coach their cricket team for the summer term I applied and got the job. It was a lovely three-month gig from April to July, which I thoroughly enjoyed as I was paid nicely as well as being given board and keep at the school. Some girls played at the school, and I picked two of them in the boys' first eleven. They did pretty well, partly thanks to the fear opposition batters had of getting out to them. One was a tidy little seamer and the other a spinner, but batters tended to pat both back and looked to score off the other bowlers. My last memory of Wellingborough was seeing Lewis Hamilton win the British Grand Prix at nearby Silverstone in early July. He'd started sixth on the grid, and the crowd went wild. Straight after, I flew to Afghanistan to take up my appointment as batting coach. This was upgraded to national coach when Kabir Khan, the former Pakistan pace bowler, left in September.

The 2015 World Cup, for which Afghanistan had qualified, was only a few months away. It was an exciting time to be head coach, and I was delighted when the Indian board gave us free use of a ground just north of Delhi where we had a month-long preparation camp for the tournament. We flew to Australia where conditions were, of course, very different and got well beaten in our opening match, by 105 runs against Bangladesh in Canberra. But a slower pitch in Dunedin in New Zealand was much more to our liking, and we gave Sri Lanka the scare of their lives. We were well-placed at 157 for three in the 33rd over thanks to a-run-a-ball fifty from Asghar Stanikzai before being bowled out for 232, which should have been more. But we took a wicket with the first ball of Sri Lanka's innings and soon had them 51 for four, which included Kumar Sangakkara's wicket. Hamid Hassan bowled him with a huge inswinger, and I remember being concerned when he celebrated it with a cartwheel. Whether that was a factor in some discomfort he experienced soon after in his left boot, I'm not sure but he did something I'd never seen before when he swapped the offending boot with Shapoor Zadran's. Shapoor later snapped Mahela Jayawardene's bat in two, but that didn't stop him scoring a brilliant hundred, his last in one-day internationals as it turned out. When Hamid had him caught at third man, Sri Lanka still needed 55 off 52 balls with four wickets in hand. We should have run out Angelo Mathews before he had faced a ball, but he and Thisara Perera, who smashed 47 not out off 26 deliveries, won it for Sri Lanka with ten balls to spare.

The narrowness of that defeat nevertheless gave us confidence going into our next game – against Scotland four days later, also in Dunedin. This was our obvious chance to record a maiden World Cup win, and when we restricted them to 210, I was confident we would chase that down. From a comfortable 85 for two, we slumped to 97 for seven, with the Scots now scenting their first World Cup in 11 attempts. Our number four, Samiullah Shenwari was still at the crease, however, and played the innings of his life to make 96 but was ninth out with 19 needed off 19 balls. In walked our number eleven, Shapoor, a big man with long hair, whose parting words as he left the dressing-room were, "Coach, I'm going to win this for you." I gave him a one in a hundred chance of doing it as he was the worst batsman I think I've ever seen in professional cricket.

I was, therefore, bracing myself for the disappointment of defeat, but thanks largely to edges, nudges and nurdles, Shapoor and Hamid somehow got the equation down to four off the last over, bowled by Iain Wardlaw. After a dot ball Shapoor set off for an unlikely single, was sent back and only survived because Matt Machan, the ex-Sussex player, missed the stumps with an underarm throw from a couple of yards. The tension was now unbearable, but it became euphoria for us when Shapoor flicked the next ball past short fine leg for four to snatch victory from the jaws of defeat. He dropped his bat and helmet before running thirty yards and going down onto his knees to give thanks to Allah.

The Scots were crestfallen but I had desperately wanted to put one over them and their Australian coach Peter Drinnen, who had succeeded me in the role. As we won, our guys were screaming and jumping up and down. The Scotland dressing-room was right next door, so I did say to our guys, "Hey, calm down, have a bit of empathy for the opposition," as I knew how down they would be feeling now. They hadn't won a game in the World Cup yet. At that stage, we weren't a full member of ICC – still an Associate – as they hadn't elevated us to Test status yet. So we and Scotland were both trying to get that nod. We were now above Scotland in the pecking order, and the favourites because we were the golden children, a country in which a war was still going on.

On the long flight from Auckland to Perth to play Australia, we had a very amusing incident. Some of the boys were nervous if there was turbulence and, when we encountered some over the Tasman Sea, Hamid Hassan screamed and grabbed my arm. I couldn't resist winding him up and told him it was a 'train-the-woman-pilot' day to see if they were good enough to take control. He started exclaiming that they couldn't use us as guinea pigs and was panicking. The other passengers thought this was hilarious, and it took Hamid three or four minutes to realise he'd been duped.

It was back to reality for us in Perth, where we suffered the biggest defeat in World Cup history in terms of runs, by 275, against Australia. It was a blisteringly hot afternoon, over 40 degrees, but we elected to bowl first in what was a day-nighter. Everyone asked me afterwards why we didn't bat first. My reasoning was that there was no way we could stop them getting whatever total we set, but we might chase say 260 if we could bowl well and keep them down to that. Frustratingly, we dropped Dave Warner in single figures before he went on to make 178 off 133 balls. One of his sixes hit a boy in the crowd of 12,000, but he later sought him out and gave him a pair of batting gloves. Poor Dawlat Zadran, who had started with a wicket maiden when he had Aaron Finch caught at slip, became only the seventh bowler in ODIs to concede over 100 runs. The Aussies' total of 417 was then the highest ever World Cup total.

The Aussies blew us away, bowling us out inside 38 overs on one of the quickest and bounciest wickets I'd seen. Mitchell Johnson was very intimidating, and Asghar was trying to back away and smash him over extra. He threw his wicket away to Johnson, who took four in total. We were skittled but the Australian public loved us, taking us to their hearts because we were the war-torn country. Everywhere we went, there were crowds of people cheering us on and giving us flowers. It was amazing the reception we were given. There are Afghans everywhere in the world, with a sizeable community in Australia. They invited us to their houses and community halls in Perth, Melbourne and Sydney, throwing parties for us, often on nights before games. I said we shouldn't go but our team manager declared, "Oh we can't turn down the generosity of these people; they want to pay homage." It was no sort of preparation for a World Cup game the next day, although the players did not touch any alcohol. I never saw one of our players drink anything alcoholic there. Legally in Afghanistan, of course, you couldn't buy alcohol, although it was available if you knew where.

From Perth it was back to New Zealand to face them in Napier. I felt no animosity from the New Zealand players. I said hello to Vettori, McCullum and the boys, as well as bowling coach Shane Bond, who was very friendly, but they just went about their business and wanted to beat us, which they did comfortably. So too did England in a rain-affected game in Sydney, where Ian Bell made an unbeaten fifty. Belly was very impressed with Hamid Hassan, who nipped it around at lively pace. He said he would be a good overseas signing for a county. Sadly for him, he ripped his knee apart trying to hurdle a boundary fence and was out for two years as a result. He's now Afghanistan's bowling coach.

A few months after the 2015 World Cup we took part in a T20 World Cup qualifying tournament in Ireland. We were strong favourites to win it along with the hosts, but after beating Netherlands and Scotland, who were the eventual joint winners as the final was washed out, we slipped up against Oman and had two other group games abandoned. We therefore finished third in our group and only qualified after beating Papua New Guinea in the play-offs. But in picking 20-year old Sharafuddin Ashraf, who took three for 27 on debut against Holland, we'd blooded a very promising left-arm spinner.

Getting younger players like him into the side was a problem, though, as none of the older ones would ever retire. Some went out of their way to block the youngsters' progress. They just made their life hell mentally. The board chairman, Nasimullah Danish, was in Ireland and got wind of some older players' behaviour and said he was disappointed with it. I told him we needed to move on two or three of the older players and find positions for them, such as coaching roles with outlying provinces in Afghanistan. They were on the decline, and I was clear we had to refresh the team. Danish, though, failed to tackle the issue and informed me that my one-year deal as national coach would not be renewed. Inzamam-ul-Haq, the former Pakistan captain, took over from me. I was retained as a coach of the Under-19s and Under-21 development squad, which was effectively a national second team. For the next two two years I would come over to Afghanistan for two-to-three-week stints prior to tournaments they played in. I would do this four or five times a year, combining the roles of batting coach, mentor and motivator for the young players.

One young batsman, Mohammad Shahzad, was probably the most talented Afghan cricketer I dealt with. There was a character, a real bobble of a guy. He was grossly overweight but had a magnificent eye. He slapped it everywhere but had no foot movement. He just thought he was the best thing in the world and refused to train. He later got dropped for being unfit, but he came back and made a one-day hundred against India. He was a real character but used to drive me insane.

Three momentous events, as far as Afghan cricket was concerned, occurred in 2017. In June of that year they were at last given full Test status by ICC. That was wonderful news for the country, along with the beneficial financial consequences, but tragedy then struck during the new two-week T20 tournament called the Shpageeza Cup that was staged in Kabul in September. That was due to have been played in July but had to be postponed when a car bomb outside the German embassy in Kabul killed 90 people.

Six teams were taking part and included two dozen or so overseas players and coaches. I had been appointed coach for a team called the Mis Ainak Knights while Adam Hollioake, the former England one-day captain, was coaching another called the Boost Defenders. Our overseas players were three Zimbabweans – Vusi Sibanda, Ryan Burl and Sikander Raza – while Adam had two South Africans in Cameron Delport and Morne van Wyk, along with the West Indian Rayad Emrit. A capacity crowd of 12,000 had packed into the national stadium for the match when, mid-way though the first innings, we heard an enormous boom from the other side of one stand.

A blast wave from the explosion shot through the stadium, and I recall my body felt like jelly. A plume of smoke rose from behind the entrance to the ground. A suicide bomber from Pakistan had tried to get into the ground, but one of the guards at a security checkpoint was suspicious of him and jumped on top of him. It was a selfless act of heroism as the bomber detonated his suicide vest, killing the guard and two others nearby. But his smothering actions saved the lives of many others. All the players hit the ground and lay flat before sprinting off into the dressing-rooms where they and support staffs stayed for what seemed an age, probably 45 minutes before the game resumed after a security sweep. I looked at Adam and said I thought it had been a bomb.

We were told a gas canister had gone off, but I knew that wasn't the case. Many of the foreign players were all saying that they were going to catch the next flight home as we were given a police escort back to the hotel. Someone from the board contacted me and said: "We can't afford to let all these players leave. You've got to help us as it will look terrible for Afghan cricket." I replied: "The first thing you have to do is admit it wasn't a gas canister. We all know it wasn't." They agreed.

Then Dean Jones, the former Australia player who had flown in from Melbourne to commentate, asked if he could have a meeting with the board. He came back from that, having negotiated an extra $5,000 on top of the basic $10,000 tournament fee for all those players or coaches who stayed on for the rest of the tournament. All of a sudden the majority of the boys changed their tune, showing how easy it was to buy players and coaches. They were also placated by a visit from the interior minister, Wais Barmak, who promised the government would ensure their safety. The majority of them stayed and completed the tournament, although Delport, who that day had scored a hundred, flew home immediately. My memories, though, are of that blast wave. All the glass shattered in the conference halls opposite the entrance to the ground. Later the Pakistan Taliban admitted responsibility for the bombing.

During the Shpageeza Cup I came across a young seamer for the first time called Naveen-ul-Haq, who performed well in it. He was appointed captain of our Under-19 side for the Asia Cup tournament for that age group that followed in November 2017 in Malaysia. He was an exceptional captain, with whom I built a very strong working relationship. As coach of the team I knew what a talented bunch they were, but they needed to be much more professional in their preparation. They responded so well that we reached the final where we met Pakistan. Batting first, we made 248 from our 50 overs, with Ikram Alikhil making an unbeaten 107. We then proceeded to skittle Pakistan out for just 63 to win the competition for the first time. Mujeeb Zadran, our mystery spinner, claimed five for 13 to take his overall tally of victims to 20 in the tournament. He went on to become the youngest player to take a five-wicket haul in a one-day international, doing so aged 17 against Zimbabwe in Sharjah, and has represented multiple franchise T20 teams including Melbourne Renegades and Mumbai Indians as well as Middlesex. Naveen, for his part, was the leading wicket-taker in the Vitality T20 Blast competition in 2022, claiming 24 victims for Leicestershire. As many as nine in that side have gone on to achieve notable success.

The Afghan Cricket Board never managed to retain national coaches for very long. Inzamam lasted about nine months before being replaced by former India batsman Lalchand Rajput. A year later Phil Simmons, the former Leicestershire and West Indies batsman, took over for the next two years but didn't visit Kabul. His successor, former South Africa all-rounder Lance Klusener, flew in once to Kabul for 24 hours but never came back again. He would meet all the teams and support staff in Dubai. The team did all right under Phil but he couldn't handle it with the senior players, as they needed moving on. Out of the blue, in October 2019, I was made chairman of selectors as well, simultaneously, as director of cricket. That meant I had actually had every job in Afghan cricket, having begun as batting coach. There were three of us on the selection committee, the other two being administrators from the provinces, but I got the side I wanted because I refused to give in. Unlike the rest of them there was no favouritism from me. They'd say something and I'd blow them out the water with cricketing logic. I was making cricketing decisions for cricketing reasons.

As chairman of selectors, I said to Phil Simmons, "What do you want? Because I didn't get that when I was coach. They were picking the senior players and their friends. That's why they got rid of me as coach; I wasn't happy with the way things were going." Phil and I worked closely together, and we dropped one of the bowlers straightaway – Dawlat Zadran – for three ODIs, three T20s and a one-off Test versus West Indies in Lucknow in India in November 2019. On hearing the news, he knocked on my door, came storming in and started bawling at me. I told him he could never do this in England and to stop, but that he was welcome to come back and ask me why he'd been left out, but that to get back into the side, he'd have to improve. He screamed: "This isn't your Afghan team; this is my team. I'm an Afghan. How dare you leave me out?" I replied: "What do you mean dare leave you out? You're already left out. Look at the team list." He then threatened he was going to come and shoot me, saying, "There are guns here; you don't know what happens." I told him to get out of my office but was now thinking, "What have I done here? He might even come and shoot me." As it happened, he never played for Afghanistan again.

A couple of months earlier in September, Rashid Khan had become the youngest Test captain in Test history – at 20 years and 350 days – for a one-off Test against Bangladesh in Chittagong. With Simmons unavailable, I was drafted in as interim coach for that mini-tour which also included a T20 triangular series with Zimbabwe. Rashid showed no signs of being burdened by the captaincy, following his half-century with 11 wickets in the match. Our victory by 224 runs was a desperately close-run thing time-wise, for we were nearly thwarted by the weather. We sat around on the fifth day waiting for the rain to stop, and when it finally relented we had 18.3 overs to take Bangladesh's last four wickets. Rashid claimed the last three with only 20 balls left of the match. The winning moment came when he had one of their specialist batsmen, Soumya Sarkar, caught at short leg, which triggered ecstatic on-field celebrations. Rashid joined Imran Khan (in 1982/83) and Allan Border (in 1988/89) as the only captains to manage a fifty and a ten-wicket match haul in the same Test. More importantly, it was our second Test win, following our maiden one against Ireland in India in March 2019.

We had hoped to make it a hat-trick of Test victories for the year against West Indies in Lucknow but batted poorly and were beaten by nine wickets. Rashid, who skippered the side again, said afterwards that he didn't want to continue as captain. He was under the influence of the much older former captain, Asghar Afghan (who had changed his surname from Stanizkai the year before). Seniority is a big thing in the Afghan community. The man with the white hair and beard is the one in charge because of his experience. You must give him respect. Rashid, although one of the best spinners in the world, was not comfortable telling Asgar what to do in the field. Although he didn't accept his demotion at the start, Asghar soon worked out he could captain the side through Rashid anyway but was re-appointed national captain in December 2019. He led the side to a 12th consecutive T20 victory over old rivals Ireland to clinch a series victory in India in March 2020. The third match, which took place one day before the World Health Organisation declared a pandemic, at last brought the Irish a consolation victory when Kevin O'Brien, needing three off the last ball of the super-over, hit Rashid for a straight six.

Considering what's sadly happened to women's opportunities in general since the Taliban took power after the Americans left Afghanistan, I was proud to help with advancing the plight of women coaches in the country. It was only when I became director of cricket that I wondered where the ladies were playing. This wasn't publicised, and there was nothing in the local papers about it. Lip service to ladies cricket was being paid. It was going on but nobody saw it. One weekend, we had brought fifteen to twenty female cricketers and coaches from around the country down to Kabul to attend a level 1 coaching course. It was organised by the woman in charge of ladies cricket, who worked out of the board's offices at the ground in Kabul. All attended in their hijabs and were quite good. Some spoke English, and others did not, but I got a translator in. We went through basics, and it was obvious they all knew about the game and had played it in whichever part of the country they came from. I was delighted to award passes to every one of them. I do wonder, though, how many of them have been allowed to coach under the new Taliban regime.

Tribute

by Naveen-Ul-Haq

Afghanistan cricketer

I have so much to say about Andy after working with him during my Under-19 years when I was captain. Under him we won the Under-19 Asia Cup, and reached the Under-19 World Cup semis for the first time. All the boys loved having him as Under-19 coach as he taught us so much and helped us to improve our games enormously.

He then became chairman of selectors and director of cricket, doing a great service to Afghanistan cricket in both jobs. What I am, and where I am today, can be traced back to what Andy did for me on my journey. I have great respect for him.

17

Living in Kabul

Several years before I arrived in 2014, the Taliban had got into the hotel where I stayed, lined up the women and children and executed them one by one. After that, security was bumped up massively with a 12-foot wall around the hotel. There were blast doors at the entry point, with room for one car only. Then there was another wall as the door closed behind, and then a second set of blast doors. Someone would check underneath every vehicle with a mirror on a stick. The security people would take all your bags and cases, which two sniffer dogs would check along with the vehicle. You would drive along another passage and through more blast doors. Dogs would then have a sniff again. You would get out and walk in through an office with scanners. Your bags would now turn up and go through an x-ray machine. Security would hand-pat you, and finally you would be allowed to pick up your bags. The vehicle would get inspected again under a roof. It would take 15 minutes to get in.

Going out, there was only one set of blast doors to get through. There were manned turrets on the wall every 50 metres with big machine guns, and on the ground military handlers with attack dogs. Eight to ten armed soldiers walked through those blast door areas. In the hotel lobby, there were three to four guys with pistols in holsters. An ex-Para in charge of security inside the hotel said that if the alarm went off, you should not open the door but go to the bathroom and lock yourself inside as there was a brick wall between the corridor and bathroom. You were then instructed to wait till Security knocked on your door, identifying themselves with an agreed codeword, and took you to a safe-room in the basement with blast-proof doors. We were all taken down there and shown this safe-room, which had its own air supply. If you were not in your room when the alarm went off, you were to make your way to the safe-room, which was for hotel residents only.

Soon after the start of my second visit, I was staying at the hotel and got a call from a member of the coaching staff. He said they were sending a car for me as it was not safe for me at the hotel that night. This jalopy arrived and I went to the ground where I slept on an inflatable swimming-pool lilo in the pavilion. It was stinking hot and the fan was clinking away. I got no sleep. The next morning they took me back to the hotel. I don't know if anything happened, but they'd been given a warning that something was going to. Members of the Taliban were embedded in the general community as it was akin to a political party. Apparently these warnings happened all the time, but it was the only one I knew about. Across the road from the hotel was the Iranian Embassy. The Iranians and Afghans didn't get on, so I suspect that it was being targeted by the Taliban.

On another night I was in bed, and I heard a whistling noise going over the hotel; it then stopped and I heard the boom of an explosion. It was a rocket, launched outside the ring of steel and fired indiscriminately to create terror. The Taliban used all sorts of means to do so. Once when we had an Under-19 camp and invited teenagers for trials, one youngster turned up an hour late for a match. I asked him where he'd been. "It was difficult to get here, sir," he explained, "as when I left my house, a body had been hung up on a lamp post in our street by the Taliban for being an informer for the Americans. The road was blocked off by the authorities, so I couldn't get out for a long time."

The only time, however, that I felt really vulnerable was when I was classified as a mere 'person' when driving to the ground. You were always in traffic jams, crawling along and then stopping. The worst thing was when you came across the massive eight-wheel troop carriers with their rotating machine-gun turrets. If you were next to it at a time when insurgents might have a crack at it, you could get caught in the crossfire. Kids would come up and throw stones at the soldier manning the machine-gun turret. Or limpet-like explosive devices might be stuck on the side of the troop carrier.

Very often I'd say to my driver to get off the road as I did not want to be travelling next to the troop carrier in a two-lane highway. You could be crawling alongside it for three kilometres. Just the thought of being close to those troop carriers was worrying. My driver did take different routes to the ground, so I got to know Kabul well with its scores of tin shacks on the side of the road selling different wares, especially green tea. Everybody drinks it in Kabul, and I even got into drinking it. It was actually quite nice. I brought back home some bags of it, and every now and then I have some to remind me of old days in Afghanistan. They drink green tea there all the time.

When I first went to Afghanistan the driver would drop me off outside the hotel, wait and watch me. I'd run across the road and through the sliding doors watched over by the turrets. I'd run in and they'd close the doors behind me. The more and more I went there, I'd get out, chat to the driver saying, "See you in the morning – 9am, ok." I'd be on the pavement, he'd drive away and other cars would come up and down, while I was still waiting for a chance to cross over. Then I'd walk across the road when there was a gap in traffic, with people milling around as I got to the door, which I'd knock on. They'd recognise me and open up in due course, but all the time I'd be vulnerable standing there on the pavement.

Once the doors had opened and closed behind me, I was safe. From taking five to ten seconds when getting out the car when there was a lull in the traffic to run across the road and get inside the closing doors, I would take two or three minutes. I just got blasé. I wouldn't have thought there were high-ranking Taliban sitting around a table discussing Andy Moles, but it's possible they did and passed their favourable judgement of me to a local warlord who, in turn, passed it down through his minions to the old cleaner in the hotel. I might be wrong but I believe it was just a friendly 'you'll be all right, don't worry' sent through a local warlord. I actually came across a couple of these warlords. Not all supported the Taliban, indeed some were government-friendly and supported the West. I met one at a gathering early on in my time there but took the advice of my brother when he advised me to stop going out as I'd get kidnapped.

My last three years there my day would be get up, watch BBC or CNN news to see what was happening in the world at large and in Afghanistan. Then it was down for breakfast before returning to my room, my phone always next to me, or going to the ground. When I was a VVIP, the hotel reception would call me to say my car had arrived, but when I was 'just' a person, my driver would ring me from outside and I'd go down in the lift, walk across the road between the traffic, nonchalantly open the door and get in. We'd then be in traffic jams for the next twenty-five to thirty minutes till we got outside the ring of steel. There were beggars everywhere – many crippled or with one leg – and once they realised it was a white man, they'd bang on the window pleading, "Money, please money." As my car crawled, they would crawl or shuffle along too. The beggars don't come anywhere near you when you're a VVIP, but when you're a mere person, you're fair game. They'd crowd around the car, and the worry was that if a Taliban terrorist saw a load of people crowding around a car, he'd know a foreigner was inside. I used to pull my hoodie over my head or wear an Afghan flat hat. Growing a beard was a good idea, too. They bought me shalwar kameez robes for one of their religious holidays, which I wore for a day. The trousers were one size-fits-all, and even on me they were way too big. You'd pull the draw string tight to hold them up. If there was no traffic, it could be as little as ten minutes to the ground, but the majority of times it was forty minutes.

Once, when the team and I had left the ground for the airport to go on a tour, the building of a radio station that was anti-Taliban was attacked and bombed only twenty minutes after we had passed it. It could have been a classic wrong-place-wrong-time scenario but luckily we were earlier – just. I followed my brother's advice closely. It was not to go to any communal places, such as coffee shops. I was out of my room only at eating times. He told me to get a doorstop, one of those rubber or wooden wedges, and put it under the door to my room. That way the door couldn't open if terrorists tried to kick it down. Apparently one guy in the Bombay Taj Hotel terrorist attack in 2008 was saved thanks to his doorstop. It's the simplest but the best precaution. I bought a pale blue wedge, and at every hotel I stayed in afterwards in Afghanistan I put it under the door.

His hotel restaurant advice was to sit where you can see people coming in. I could see through a decorative alcove if there was a commotion and had a wall behind me so that no one could attack me from behind. The waiters came through a door to my right, and I knew that would be my escape route as there was always a way out through the kitchen. Or a bit further down the passage from the dining-room was the safe-room. So if something happened, I could jump through the alcove and get to the safe-room or could exit through the kitchen.

It was all day in the hotel room for me on off-days. I did at times get cabin fever, but I'm quite good at compartmentalising things. It was my choice; I'd decided to be there. I was getting paid reasonably well, and it's turned out that the money I earned in Afghanistan has enabled me to get by after what's happened with my leg. I've had five years of unemployment since it was amputated, although the part-time Bahamas work has been a godsend.

One time when things weren't so great between me and the CEO, Shafiqullah Stanikzai, he wanted to save on my hotel costs. He proposed I stay instead inside the ground in the academy's accommodation, which was dirty and horrible. I told him I wasn't prepared to do that and called my brother, who got hold of a private security company that offered accommodation in Kabul. It was like an Airbnb except that it was run by ex-military personnel. My brother said he could get the Afghan Cricket Board a deal where it was half the price of the hotel, with food and board included. So I stayed there for a while – and I loved it. There was beer if you wanted it, roast beef with Yorkshire pudding, pork sausages and bacon for breakfast which you couldn't get at the hotel. It was like an English guesthouse, but it was just a house in a built-up neighbourhood, with walls of sandbags surrounding it. Outside those there were other compartments where the guards stayed overnight, all manned by heavily armed ex-military. They used to tan themselves on the roof; it was a bit like a holiday home. Word of what might be happening was relayed to these hard ex-soldiers, who lived life to the full, having a couple of whiskies at night. The board, though, decided they were happier with me in the hotel than in an army house and moved me back there after ten days, even if the hotel cost them twice as much. But it was a lovely little break, and to have sausages and bacon for breakfast was just unbelievable. The military guys had taught the Afghan house lady how to make things like cottage pie, and it was very much like Little England in the middle of Afghanistan.

Every night I'd come home after leaving the ground between 6 and 7pm when nets finished, and there'd be an English meal. Gammon and pineapple with mashed potato was another specialty of hers. I also enjoyed the company of the soldiers, although I didn't really get on with one guy when they found out I was there thanks to my brother, who knew one of the main bosses. This guy, a Scot, thought I was a plant from head office. "What do you mean I'm a plant?" I asked him. "I know you are," he replied. "Why are you here if you're not one?" "Because I coach cricket," I retorted. "No, you're here to rat on us," he declared. "What are you doing then?" I fired back at him. "See, why are you asking questions like that?" he responded. He thought I was there to tell his bosses what they got up to, but I didn't see them get up to anything.

The house had about six bedrooms, and there was a Swede working for his government, a Dane working for an NGO and another English guy who was working in IT. It was interesting being there and like a breath of fresh air. There was no light around it at night, and you drove down alleyways wide enough for a car and a half to get there. You could have been ambushed there, but at the top of the road for the whole of this residential area was a boom with armed guards, who checked every car coming in. We were at the end of the lane in what was effectively a dead-end. The house was protected by a wall of sandbags with a machine gun sticking out of a hole in it, and guys monitoring the road so that they would be ready to take on fire. Inside, all the operatives carried their rifles and other weapons. Their vests and their helmets were at the door so that if anything happened they could put them on. At all times, even if they went to the toilet, they had their guns ready. I enjoyed it, but it was also good to get back to the hotel as I'd had enough of this guy who insisted I was a plant. He got a little bit vindictive with things he'd say in front of the others, who would tell him to leave me alone.

18

Amputation

The saga of my left leg all started just before we went for the tour of Bangladesh. We decided the heat of UAE would be good preparation as we knew Chittagong would be very hot. Our fitness trainer, Jason, suggested going for a walk in Abu Dhabi for about half an hour as I'd said I wanted to get a bit fitter. I wore no socks, just trainers. It was the middle of the day, and scorching hot, and I remember thinking, "Bloody hell, this pavement is hot, and my foot's burning." Anyway, we got back to the hotel, where I had a shower and sat down. I looked at the floor, and there was blood everywhere. On the ball of my left foot, the skin had gone and there was a big blister. So I called our team doctor, who came and had a look. "Moler, that's not good," he said. "We need to go to hospital and get it checked out, and get it dressed as you're a diabetic." So they cleaned it at the hospital, and the doctor said I might need a skin graft, adding that every time I walk around, the skin and plaster will come off. I was diagnosed with diabetes in 1986 when I got thirsty and dizzy. I have had to inject insulin four times a day since then.

We were in UAE for another five days or so, then went to Bangladesh for the Test. Every day during it, I went to the hospital for the foot to be dressed but the doctor there eventually advised that he needed to do a skin graft. Skin was taken off my inner thigh. I was in hospital for about seven to eight days in Dhaka, causing me to miss the T20 triangular tournament after the Test. The team left and went home, but I was still in hospital. The doctor who looked after me in the English military hospital in Dhaka was brilliant. From there I went home to Cape Town for a month, where the skin graft was starting to heal. Then came the match against West Indies in Lucknow, for which the team doctor said he could get me a moon boot to walk around in. This seemed ideal, but the locally-made Afghan moon boot had padding that was rudimentary.

My little toe rubbed on the fibre glass of the boot but because I've got neuropathy, through being a diabetic, I have no feeling in my toes. They are numb. I could see there was a red mark on the side of my little toe but thought it a blister. A sore developed. When it was eventually discovered, the team doctor cleaned it every day and poured iodine on it. After Lucknow we went to India where I prepared the team until Lance Klusener arrived in the New Year to take over as head coach. I'd applied for that job but to keep me sweet they gave me the role of director of cricket, which was a puppet appointment. At least they paid me more money, which I've been living on. From there, I came back to Cape Town. Before I left, our team doctor told me to go and see my doctor in Cape Town, adding he wasn't happy with the state of the toe and that I needed to get it looked at properly.

I flew in to Cape Town during the evening and went straight to the doctor the next morning. She saw me hobbling in in my moon boot, said it didn't look very good and took a swab, sending it off in a jar for analysis. The phone went just after one o'clock that afternoon, and I was told to return straightaway to the hospital as I needed intravenous antibiotics as soon as soon as possible to counter a nasty infection. When I got there, a special poultice was applied to draw it out and I was told I must stay in the hospital for five days while the intravenous antibiotics were administered. I had two specialist orthopaedic surgeons in to see me. One said he thought we could save the toe, but the other was concerned it might drop off because the blood supply was not great. That's something that happens apparently.

I did the five days in Louis Leipoldt Hospital and was sent home with more antibiotics, with a review of my situation set for three days later. That night, however, I woke up in the middle of it, sweating profusely with my leg throbbing. It was bright red and swollen beneath the knee. I went back to hospital in the morning, and they decided to keep me in, this time in a room by myself. Before, I'd been in a ward with four others. My partner Megan thought it was strange I was in my own room, but I was quite happy not to have to put up with the noise of other people. Another doctor then arrived – one I hadn't seen before – who was the head specialist for ankles, shins and feet. He was a brilliant doctor, an awesome guy, and said: "I don't like the look of what's going on here. I think we'll have to remove your toe. I'm afraid we can't save it."

So they removed the toe. I imagined they would just cut the toe off and nothing else, but they actually cut in a line straight down. I lost a quarter of my foot. They then stitched it loosely in such a way that it was still open and air could get in. They said: "We'll send you home for another four to five days and hopefully it'll recover." Two days later, however, I woke up in the middle of the night and it was roaring again. So I returned to hospital that morning and was seen by the head specialist. He said: "Andy, I'm going to come back tomorrow for a final look, but I need to let you know that we are probably going to have to cut your foot off below the knee. You have a germ in there that's eating away at your flesh, and we've got to get ahead of it. We tried to catch it by taking your toe off, but it had got further than we thought into your foot. We can take off another couple of toes if you want, but I'll talk to you tomorrow morning about it. Right now I just want you to process what might happen to you."

He was brilliant, with a great bedside manner. The next morning at about 6.30, he came to say hello and revealed they had taken a swab in the night while I was sleeping. "My recommendation is that you need to have the amputation." I thought for a second and replied: "Well, you wouldn't tell me how to play a forward defensive stroke, would you, so I'm not going to tell you what to do with my leg. If it's your recommendation that this has to happen, let's get it done. When can you do it?" He replied: "Twelve o'clock today." I said: "OK, put me down." So I rang Megan and told her, and then called my father and Tim Munton. My brothers and my sons were informed. Only Megan had known how serious my situation was, and I hadn't wanted my sons to know so hadn't told them.

I was now preparing myself mentally for the operation, with no breakfast allowed. While I was waiting, I heard a commotion and wondered what was going on. It was the start of lockdown. That very morning, South Africa went into lockdown because of Covid. At 11.30 the nurses came to get me and wished me luck. I remember being wheeled down to theatre and hearing them say what they were going to do to me. There was a lot of legal stuff – what are you here for, what's going to happen, what you think is going to happen and which leg they're going to amputate. They do it step-by-step and you confirm step-by-step. Then I had that lovely milky juice stuff injected into my arm to knock me out. Megan called it the Michael Jackson juice. You just felt on top of the world. When you wake up, you're 'Wahoo' – on another planet – and it's the most magnificent feeling except they were doing it to take my leg off.

I woke up after the operation back in my room in a tent-like covering. Megan, who'd had to push her way past security because of the new Covid restrictions, was allowed to see me for a short time and showed me the photos of the leg post-amputation. She was then kicked out and I was lying there, occasionally pressing the morphine drip, when the pain became too much, although the amount was limited so that I couldn't overdose. Suddenly I saw these bodies, some two at a time, being wheeled past the entrance to my room and wondered what was going on. Later, there was another one and then three or four at the same time. They had died from Covid. And I suddenly started talking to myself: "Why are you feeling sorry for yourself? You've lost half a leg. What's your problem? I've seen half a dozen bodies going past. F***ing grow up. Come on, sort yourself out. Live your life. Why are you worried about it? It's not the end of the world." I was employed by the ACB, who were still paying me. But I couldn't travel due to Covid, and I couldn't travel because of this anyway.

The Afghans paid me for another three months, and then I got a one-line email from the chairman: "Please be advised that your employment by Afghan Cricket is no longer needed." That was it – bang. The last communication I ever had from them. I got sent home two days after the operation, and Megan looked after me fantastically. All I'd got was some crutches which I had to learn to use. Three or four days later, Megan drove me back to see the surgeon. There was not a car on the roads as no one was allowed out. The surgeon looked at it and said he was really pleased with the way it was. It was re-dressed, and I went back again a few days later. On the third visit back, the stitches were taken out, and it then healed. They gave me a device called a vacuum patch, where you wear a little motor on your belt, which draws air out of a plastic bag sealed around the wound. The idea is to keep it permanently pressed against it so as to prevent infection. The big fear was if I got an infection in that cut, they'd have to cut it off above the knee. Every time, they tried to pull the bag off, it stuck to the dried blood and the wound started bleeding again. It was very sore, but the device was a great tool to help prevent infection. Gradually, though, it got better and better, and I think I was on crutches until July.

Then I went to see a specialist that makes prosthetic legs. I was made a plastic one to start off so that I'd get used to it. Initially I needed a walking frame to assist me but when I could walk without it, they made me another one. They have to do that because the stump shrinks when the remains of the calf muscle waste away with no foot beneath it. As a result, the stump becomes looser and looser over time in the cup at the top of the prosthetic leg. The cup is made to fit like a glove but over time it needs to be reduced in size. Each cup costs around £2,000. It's a long process, getting the leg made and getting used to walking on it. When I got the final fitting, the insurance company refused to pay for the medical bills in South Africa which I'd already settled as you had to pay up front. They claimed it was a diabetic incident, but I informed them it wasn't as I had had an MRSA infection. Diabetes didn't help, but diabetes wasn't the reason why I had my leg amputated.

My close mate of many years, Tony Finch, fixed up a lawyer in London, who took my case on for free and fought them for about eight months. The company kept refusing to pay before finally relenting, but at this point a new handler took the case on and said they wouldn't pay after all. In the end, however, perhaps because they realised that running with it was costing them more, they eventually did pay my bills as well as giving me £3,000 for discomfort. I'd already paid out R400,000 (about £18,000) of my own money to cover the cost of the ops. Then I had to get the leg built, and luckily the PCA very very kindly came forward through David Graveney, who rang me. They then got hold of Megan's number through Tim Munton without telling me, rang her and asked, "What do you need?" She wasn't sure what to tell them but mentioned we'd just had to buy a special seat and rail for the shower, as well as a few simple things to help with my mobility. "Right, send us the bill, we'll pay for all that," the PCA told her. They then got hold of me and said that when the leg was made up, to send them the bills. They covered everything.

Around four to five months after my op, the PCA were running a 'Ten for 10' scheme to raise money for their general charity fund. Give a tenner to do ten things was the idea. To help them back, I said I'd walk 10,000 metres. Although I'd only just got my Zimmer frame, I pledged to walk twice round the block here in our housing estate north of Cape Town. That's 600 metres. The next day I'd walk somewhere else, maybe on the beach front, and add up my metres in increments till I'd done 10,000 metres. I raised £15,000, all of which went to the PCA. They gave me £10,000 all in all to pay for this, and I gave them £15,000 back.

I completed the walk at the end of the South African winter. It took about a month as at first I could only walk 50 yards. It got me out of the house and raised money for a great cause to help fellow pros. I wanted to give something back, but it also gave me more confidence as you have to learn how to walk again. Things like getting up out of a chair are not straightforward. There was no pain from the scarring or the joint, but the bottom of the stump is quite soft – not raw, but like a soft piece of skin. That has to harden up like the heel on your foot. And the prosthetic leg is like a brand new pair of shoes. So when you start walking again, the bottom of the stump has to get used to the cup where it rubs. If there are any sores, you have to stay off your leg as the chance of infection again is massive.

So it's quite a process you have got be aware of. The guys who made the prosthetic were brilliant. I could go back and talk to them any time, and they'd make slight adjustments to help. But you've got to break the stump in. When you first get it made, it's tight, fitting like a glove, as they take a plastercast of your stump and create a mould of it. Then they make the plastic leg, but the stump immediately starts to shrink. So you then need to use a sock around the stump to pad it out to fit. After about two months they replaced the plastic cup with a fibreglass one, which is rock hard. You can't damage it. My first one lasted about two years before the stump shrinkage becomes such you need to go back and get the whole process repeated, with a new plaster cast and a new mould. I'm still using that second one, but it's starting to get loose and will last only till early 2026 I think. They cost about £8,000. The PCA have said they'll help in future. About six to eight months ago,

I needed a new silicon sleeve which cost about £1,000. They paid for that a few days after I rang them. They are a wonderful organisation and look after anybody who's played one-first class game. I daresay they can't support everything, but they try to cover you and look after you. I intend to try to help them again in the future.

During that first year I constantly got cuts and sores in the stump as you walk differently to before. You don't have the same gait. There's no feeling in the prosthetic, and you trip over as a result. If you bump into a stone or a crack in the pavement, normally you can feel it through your toes. On my left side you feel nothing. On about three or four occasions, I've tripped and fallen over which is very embarrassing, but my character just doesn't want people to help me get up off the street. But I need help when that happens; you just can't get up. If I fall in the house, Megan just brings me a dining-room chair and I can get my hands on that to get myself up. Twice I've fallen in supermarket carparks where, if you don't see a stone or a crack, you can go over. That's the reason why I walk with my head down, looking for stones, cracks, kerbs and drain covers. They're all a potential danger. But people have come to help.

In Cape Town, where I live, they're not as geared up for handicapped people as in the UK, but the UK has also got lots of issues in that respect when I visit there. Stairs to shopping centres or restaurants often have no rails on the walls, for example. I have to do one step at a time because the prosthetic leg doesn't bend at the ankle. I also have to go up sideways rather than straight on. I remember once tripping with my good foot on a top step and falling over. Megan came rushing over but I shouted, "Get away from me, get away from me, I don't need help." I did, of course, and I apologised to her, but I felt intense frustration as you just want to be independent so badly. Now I am pretty independent, but I still need help every now and then. Five years or so on, I've got used to it and haven't fallen over for two or three years now.

When I go out, I plot subconsciously where I'm going. Because of the strength of the rain in Cape Town when it does rain, the drains and the gutters are enormous. So when I cross a road, I look for the smallest step up because if you take a big step the balance has to be perfect. The hardest thing is stepping down off a big step. Getting up and down off a bus, which I do the whole time in my current part-time role coaching the Bahamas cricket team, is very difficult. Getting off a bus, you're stepping down probably two feet as the team bus doesn't lower down like some of the buses in England. I was in Argentina in late 2024 for a tournament with the Bahamas, and we travelled everywhere in a 48-seater bus. I don't want to hit the ground first with my prosthetic leg as it will bounce. I have to go down sideways with the good leg first, but I'm almost doing the splits in the process. Then you swing the prosthetic over. With practice you find a way, but in places like Argentina and South Africa and, I daresay, on some buses in the UK, there's no lowering. They need to bring that in to make like easier for the handicapped.

Now I have no pain at all. The only thing that does happen is that if I have to walk any serious distance, and by that I mean 150 to 200 metres, I get problems with my glutes in my good leg. To be honest, I need to work on my fitness to help, but I've come to the realisation, and I hate to admit it, that I am an invalid now. I do only have one leg, but that leg allows me to live a life. I can walk in a mall for, let's say, 20 minutes, then I have to sit down for about ten minutes to allow my good leg, glutes and lower back to get better. Then I get up and I can walk for another 15 minutes. Yes, it has impaired my mobility – and I obviously can't jog any more – but I can get to the shops, I've found a way to get up steps to go to restaurants, I can live a normal life and I can drive. Thankfully I lost my left leg which means I can drive an automatic car. If it had been my right leg, then you have to get cars reconfigured for you.

Unfortunately my brother Paul lost his right leg after he was sunbathing in Spain. He had a snooze in the afternoon on a sun-lounger and didn't put any sun cream on the top of his foot. He got severely sunburnt on it. The skin blistered and those blisters got infected and, because he'd been a diabetic since he was eight years old, his neuropathy was a lot worse than mine. His blood supply wasn't as strong as those who don't have diabetes, and that's why he had his leg amputated. To help him get over it, as he lives on his own in Birmingham, I flew to the UK in early 2023 to stay with him for three months. Mentally he struggled for about six weeks to come to terms with the fact he was an amputee. Whereas I was released from hospital two days after my op, the NHS wouldn't let him go home for twelve months as they said his house wasn't fit for an amputee. He was put in a care home for the majority of that time. He had to rent a bungalow which had wide enough doorways and no stairs. Once has was there, he was much happier as he was with his dog and had his independence. But he really struggled with blisters and had to go back in twice from the care home to the hospital to receive antibiotics intravenously. They just couldn't stop his stump getting infected.

We look a right pair now when we go the pub together … we can make a pair of good legs between us! I often joke we should go and buy a pair of shoes as we have the same size foot. I'll have the right one, and he can have the left one. He's got over it now. He works for Land Rover as an IT specialist, working from home, and is fine. Like me, though, he had to come to the realisation this is what it is, to stop feeling sorry for yourself, start realising that there is a life ahead and acknowledge that you have to let people help you. Like me he's stubborn and proud. He scoots around his house in a wheelchair, only putting his prosthetic on when he goes out of the house. By contrast I put mine on when I get up, I keep it on all day and only take it off when I go to bed at night. What I did do for him was organise two fund-raising dinners after the NHS told him he'd have to wait 18 to 24 months for his prosthetic leg. Tim Munton, not just my greatest mate but a wonderful man, arranged for one of Paul's mates, who sings in a band, to perform at Moseley CC, my old club. They kindly said we could have the facilities for free, and the place was packed out, absolutely rammed with over 200 people. Tim, Gladstone Small and I gave some stuff for auction, and Warwickshire donated some memorabilia they had. We raised four to five thousand pounds. Then, a month later, Moseley gave us the club facilities again and we had a Q&A with Ashley Giles and Asif Din with Munts compering. That raised another three to four thousand. There was a go-fund-me page that his daughters set up, raising the overall total to over £10,000, which paid for his leg. Instead of having to wait two years in a wheelchair for the basic NHS ankle and foot model, with no movement at all, he was able to afford to get the high quality leg I have.

The biggest challenge is the mental side of it. When I saw those bodies being wheeled past my room just after my operation, I made a mental switch straightaway. "Stop feeling sorry for yourself," I said out loud as it wasn't the end of the world. It's difficult, and I've realised as I've applied for a few jobs that nobody really wants a one-legged coach. Not even the England Disability team. Eighteen months after I had the amputation, I applied for it through Ashley Giles, the ECB cricket director. He, like all my old team-mates, had got in touch and was fantastic, asking if I was all right and if he could help in any way. I said to him, "What about your England Disability team? Surely I could be a good fit, couldn't I?" Ashley agreed it was a good idea and gave me the number of the person who oversaw the disability team. So I rang him, and he said they'd love to have me help them when they practise on Sundays in the cricket season on different club grounds. When I questioned why they didn't practise more often, he replied that they didn't get enough funding to do so. He ended by saying he could offer me three hours pay per week as there was no money to employ coaches. Perhaps that's something the ECB could look at. You see the money being splashed around by them and wonder why they can't do more for the invalids around the country who want to play a sport like cricket.

The stump fits into the fibreglass pocket. There's a ratchet system, a spike with grooves, that connects and gives you full confidence that you can take a step and that the prosthetic won't be left behind you. Now I can attach it with my eyes closed whereas before it would take me a minute or more to affix. Then you've got the aluminium rod that comes out the bottom into the ankle joint. At the bottom of the foot part is a loop that gives you suspension and some cushioning (which is why it's so expensive). Mine is split like a hoof. The bottom, called the sports option, is good if you can play golf. I used to play it at every opportunity and was a 7-handicapper. I haven't played for six years, which kills me, but you have to come to terms with what you can and can't do. I can rock slowly thanks to the sports option. Without that cushioning you'd just go 'clunk, clunk' when you walk and that vibration would go up into your stump, which would be awful. That's what the basic NHS leg offers you. Paul has an upgraded one as his was fitted in early 2024, for technology has improved them in the four years since mine was first fitted. In two years' time they'll be better again. I'd just replace the shell as the whole lot is 12 to 15 thousand pounds. Sometimes to get up a big step, if there are no rails, I have to put my hand on someone's shoulder. But I want to emphasise I've learnt how to live with it, and I live a full life. The only issue is I've been unemployed for five years, apart from the part-time work I do for the Bahamas. I've had to use my savings and am looking forward to reaching 66 in February 2027 when I'll get two-thirds of my British pension.

Tribute

by Brand van den Heever

Certified Prosthetist & Orthotist, Cape Town

I first met Andy on May 8th 2020. Covid had just reared its ugly and controversial head. Being as involved with cricket as he was, I must regrettably say I did not initially know too much about Andy's past. A quick google session and I was up to speed with the man I was dealing with. To no surprise I realised that google can give you facts and accomplishments, but it cannot show you a person's grit and determination.

Andy had come to my practice seeking a quote for a transtibial (below knee) prosthesis for his leg. He had lost his left leg due to complications arising from an MRSA infection.

As a positive person with a great vibe, Andy was welcomed into our family at Orthocare in Cape Town immediately. His entire mindset was just right from the start. It is impossible to fail if you have this mindset, especially in his situation. That is just the person he is.

Initially we fitted him with a test prosthesis to see how the residual limb would hold up. He aced the testing stages, and we proceeded to make him a final prosthesis. We made him what was (and still is) a high-end prosthesis so that he could still continue to pursue his coaching career in international cricket. His prosthesis would afford him the opportunity to have shock absorption as well as rotation to be able to move as comfortably as possible. The socket was made of carbon fibre to give the greatest strength at the lowest weight.

Andy took to the prosthesis like a duck to water. He mastered it in a very short time and the next thing was that he launched the 'Moler's Marathon' to benefit the Professional Cricketers' Association. There is just no stopping this man.

Andy also expressed the need for a water prosthesis (a prosthesis that you are able to use in a shower, for instance). This is something not a lot of amputees have access to, and it makes the world of difference to have something like that available. It was a request he put in the first day we met. Of course, Andy got what he wanted and the rest is history.

It has to be said that it is not always moonlight and roses when it comes to wearing and operating a prosthesis. Andy has had issues with skin breakdown and pressure sores, to name a few. The thing that sets Andy apart is he does not pitch up to our practice with a defeatist attitude. He makes an appointment, states his requirement and trusts us to sort it out, which has been the case up to this point. He has dominated any setbacks he has had with his prosthesis like a champion.

Andy is also not just a patient that comes to me when he needs assistance. He brought me a bottle of wine from the Hemel-en-Aarde Valley in the western Cape just because he could. He did not have to come in for anything prosthesis related; he just dropped in to bring me an undeserved spoil. Andy is a man of great taste and an absolute pleasure to deal with. I can honestly say that I would have a pint of beer with this man any day of the week. Cheers to you, Andy!

19

Uzbekistan

Six months or so after my operation in 2020, I got a phone call from the Afghan Under-19 coach, asking if I would like to come to Uzbekistan shortly before Christmas. He'd got to know the Uzbek cricket chairman, a wealthy petro-chemist, who had fallen in love with cricket while a student in India. At the time Uzbekistan were not a member of ICC but, winding the clock on, they are now an Associate member. They joined at the very bottom of world cricket, and they are trying to grow.

"Moler, I'm up in Uzbekistan," he said. "I've had a word with the boss, and we need to do a level 1 coaching course for a few locals so we can get them into the schools and start cricket here. I've told him about you, and he says he'll fly you up for a week to conduct the course." I immediately thought: "Bloody hell, Uzbekistan, what's it going to be like there? And how am I going to go on a flight with my leg?" But I'm a sucker for travel and love going to new places, so I told them I'd come.

I got on a plane to Dubai and overnighted there at an airport hotel. I didn't take the leg off as your ankles swell when you fly. I thought the stump would swell and I'd never get the leg back on again. In the event, the stump was tighter, but it wasn't too bad. I got wheelchair assistance to the front of the airport queues. All those queues for passport control or boarding, I don't do them any more now. I always sit with the aisle on the left so that my left leg can swing into it once the flight's underway. I eventually got into Uzbekistan at 2am. The wind was blowing, and there was snow on the ground. I got through immigration and there was a group of people waving placards with 'Welcome, Coach Andy' on them. "Bloody hell," I thought. These people are waiting with great big fur coats on and big mitts. To them it was just another night out in the elements but it was Baltic cold, with it being mid-December. I just had a cap and a puffer jacket. They took me to the hotel which was very nice. I walked in there, and unlike Afghanistan there was beer available. They'd stocked the fridge with Heinekens. They made me feel so welcome. I was told that if I wanted anything, just to sign for it and they would pay. I didn't actually drink much beer because I'd gone off it a bit, compared to my early years.

The next morning they asked if we would could start the level one course straightaway. I went through the basics: stance, grip, backlift; holding the seam, seam position, spinning the ball; fielding. There were twelve locals, made up of five women and seven men, but they didn't look too sporty. One of them was an Olympic judo medal winner who coached judo; two others were boxing coaches; then there was someone from the football federation; another from the fencing association. All Olympic coaches. We were in a boardroom-type enclosure, where I said, "OK, tell me what you know about the game." Blank faces stared back at me. Not a word. It transpired they hadn't even seen a game of cricket. They didn't know anything about it, not even that there's three stumps or a bat and ball. They'd been roped in as they were Olympic coaches.

We went on to a tennis stadium where the flooring and lights were top-class, but it had open sides and it was freezing. People were running around with their coats on. I started off just hitting the ball, and laughing and joking. It was like working with five-year old kids. They had got no idea; some batted one-handed and others hoicked across the line with no hand-eye coordination whatever. But I got a lot of fun into it. I thought it might be a good idea to show them some action on YouTube of England or Afghanistan playing. They loved it! Now it was time to explain the game of cricket, but of course they just went blank, having no idea what I was talking about. So there was no way I could do a Level 1 course, and in addition they were not part of the ICC. I was thinking this was going to be a long week.

All I did was show them videos every morning for five days, and in the afternoon I tried some very basic technical things. I didn't show forward defensives or anything like that. The chairman was around although he would go off, leaving his eight-year-old son. Four people actually managed to embrace the rudimentary concepts. Others had no idea. I tried to get the quartet to explain things to the others in their own language. They did improve to a degree, but at the end I said I couldn't give them a level 1 certificate, merely an attendance certificate, and those there did go back and introduce the game to the schools. I was also taken to a university where I gave a speech to an audience of 200 or more women.

Since my visit they have got the game off the ground and have actually played some T20 competitions there, getting some players in from Pakistan. They are building a ground, and a group of Pakistani coaches and an Indian have been spending time there. The chairman has done a wonderful job, and all with his own money. I see their progress on Facebook every now and then, and think they have an agreement with Pakistan that they will help them. A groundsman was sent to teach them how to prepare a ground, although they have an artificial wicket.

Uzbekistan struck me as an immaculately clean ex-Soviet state. They have four or five-lane highways, and no army as such. Muslims, Christians and Jews live together there, and all get on. It was just refreshing to be in that part of the world and see how people can live together. I ended up thoroughly enjoying the week, if not the cricketing part. How was I supposed to get the judo coach to persuade his charges to play cricket? But cricket has grown tremendously, and they have had players from neighbouring Afghanistan over. The swelling in my leg was something of a problem, and I ended up sleeping with the prosthetic on. It got hard to take it off, and I was worried I couldn't get it back on again. But most importantly, I now knew I could travel, which was a huge boost to morale. Not many people have been to Uzbekistan, so that was also a plus for me.

20

The Bahamas

After my amputation I applied for a couple of jobs: at Warwickshire to be their pathway development coach as well as another position in Sri Lanka. I didn't get an interview for either. But Andy Pick rang me out the blue one day, saying the president of the Bahamas Cricket Association, Greg Taylor, was going to call me about going there for three months to prepare them for the American qualifiers for the T20 World Cup. Picky had met Taylor during a sabbatical in the Americas as the ICC's development officer for the two continents. Half an hour later, the phone went and it was Greg. "Hi Andy, we're looking for a coach, and Picky, whom I respect, says you're my man." I cut in: "Well, let me stop you there before you go any further. I'm going to be upfront with you. You do know that I've only got one leg, don't you?" His exact words were: "I don't want you to play, Andy. I want you to coach. I want what's in your head, not what's in your leg." And we've become great friends since; I've been back there several times now. People shouldn't get the idea I'm sitting on the beach sipping Pina Coladas, staying in a five-star hotel. I stay in an Airbnb arrangement at the back of Taylor's house in Nassau. But they look after me magnificently and are lovely people.

In August 2021, sixteen months after my leg was amputated, I flew to Dubai, then New York and onto the Bahamas for three months preparation there ahead of the tournament. That was in Antigua in November. We didn't play very well, though, and didn't qualify. US and Canada were the two best teams, ahead of the likes of us, Mexico and Argentina. All the countries were able to stay in one resort with Covid jab certificates. I was frustrated as the players wanted to belt every ball for six. Their standard was decent cub cricket but nowhere near top club cricket like the Birmingham League. We had three or four dangerous players and, if all were at their best, we could compete. Canada and US played the final, which the Americans won. Both qualified, though.

Canada thought they had won when the wicketkeeper caught the last American batsman and threw the ball high in the air and the whole team celebrated in a huddle. The umpire, however, gave it not out and the Americans ran two while the ball was lying at mid-wicket. Then all hell broke loose. They were the best two teams by far, with Bermuda the third best.

There were no tournaments in 2022, but at the end of it Taylor rang to ask me if I could go back to the Bahamas in early 2023 for another three months to prepare for the next T20 qualifying tournament. This time it was in Argentina. Returning to Buenos Aires brought back nice memories of my time coaching at a school there for four months in the 1991 winter. This time we did better but finished fifth or sixth. On low, slow turning wickets, our guys found it hard as they are brought up on artificial wickets. But the next time we played a tournament in Argentina, in late 2024, we selected five spinners in out squad, batted much better and finished third out of eight behind Cayman Islands and Bermuda. The top three qualified to go into a four-team play-off league with hosts Canada in mid-2025. The winners of that go to India for the next T20 World Cup in 2026, with Canada strong favourites.

21
Blessed by family

I look back now with immense gratitude and pride that I was able to follow my dream to be a successful county cricketer for Warwickshire. It was all I wanted to do from the age of 20, and to follow twelve years as a pro with nearly thirty as a coach has been a real privilege. I've been fortunate to travel the world, experience many different cultures, meet some outstanding human beings and make some special friendships. Yes, there was some rotten luck with losing my left leg, but I've come to terms with it and continue to live life to the full.

Above all, I'm grateful to have brought up two sons successfully and to have found a special second partner in Megan Farrelly, who has been heroically supportive since I lost my leg. I was lucky enough to educate both my boys, Danny and Matthew, at one of South Africa's top schools, Grey College in Bloemfontein, where they loved sports and lent more towards football than cricket. Both seem to have inherited my wanderlust, for Danny, who went into the restaurant trade, now lives in France with his French wife, while Matthew, who is a teacher, is based in China, where he is engaged to a Chinese girl. We remain a close family, despite living in different continents. I have a very amicable relationship with my former wife, Jacqui, who lives in Bloemfontein, and is very supportive of the boys. A curious irony is that Megan's former husband, Mark Farrelly, is my best mate in South Africa. For all my trials and tribulations, I could hardly have lived a fuller life.

CAREER STATISTICS

All figures are from the Cricket Archive website

FIRST-CLASS CRICKET

BATTING AND FIELDING

M	I	NO	Runs	HS	Ave	100	50	Ct
230	416	40	15,305	230*	40.70	29	89	146

BOWLING

Overs	Mdns	Runs	Wkts	Best	Ave
566	121	1882	40	3/21	47.05

SEASON-BY-SEASON FIRST-CLASS BATTING

	M	I	NO	Runs	HS	Ave	100	50
ENGLAND								
1986	11	18	3	738	102	49.20	2	5
1987	25	46	3	1431	151	33.27	4	4
1988	18	31	2	968	115	33.37	1	5
1989	21	38	5	1138	130*	24.48	2	8
1990	24	46	8	1854	224*	48.78	4	10
1991	22	39	2	1246	133	33.67	1	10
1992	23	41	3	1359	122	35.76	1	12
1993	19	34	3	1228	117	39.61	2	8
1994	11	20	3	863	203*	50.76	1	5
1995	9	16	-	710	131	44.37	1	6
1996	13	25	-	903	176	36.12	2	4
1997	12	22	3	635	168	33.42	1	2
Total	**208**	**376**	**35**	**13073**	**224***	**38.33**	**22**	**79**
SOUTH AFRICA								
1986/87	7	12	1	705	174	64.09	3	2
1987/88	6	12	2	657	200*	65.70	3	2
1988/89	6	11	1	627	230*	62.70	1	3
1991/92	1	2	1	91	88*	91.00	-	1
1992/93	1	1	-	59	59	59.00	-	1
1994/95	1	2	-	93	83	46.50	-	1
Total	**22**	**40**	**5**	**2232**	**230***	**63.77**	**7**	**10**

ONE-DAY (LIST A) CRICKET

BATTING AND FIELDING

M	I	NO	Runs	HS	Ave	100	50	Ct
185	177	8	4733	127	28.00	2	35	50

BOWLING

Overs	Mdns	Runs	Wkts	Best	Ave
160.2	2	834	12	2/24	69.50

SEASON-BY-SEASON ONE-DAY BATTING

	M	I	NO	Runs	HS	Ave	100	50
ENGLAND								
1986	12	9	2	156	85	22.28	-	1
1987	20	19	-	520	127	27.36	1	3
1988	14	14	-	340	79	24.28	-	2
1989	13	13	-	273	65	21.00	-	2
1990	11	10	-	425	81	42.50	-	5
1991	22	21	2	660	93*	34.73	-	6
1992	25	25	1	698	96*	29.08	-	6
1993	20	19	-	396	66	20.84	-	2
1994	5	5	2	205	105*	68.33	1	-
1995	11	11	-	430	90	39.09	-	4
1996	12	11	1	177	36	17.70	-	-
1997	9	9	-	250	64	27.77	-	3
Total	**174**	**166**	**8**	**4530**	**127**	**28.67**	**2**	**34**
SOUTH AFRICA								
1986/87	3	3	-	36	21	12.00	-	-
1987/88	5	5	-	121	50	24.20	-	1
1988/89	3	3	-	46	34	15.33	-	-
Total	**11**	**11**	**-**	**203**	**50**	**18.45**	**-**	**1**

INNINGS OF 150+ IN FIRST-CLASS CRICKET

230*	Griqualand West v Northern Transvaal B	Centurion Park	1989
224*	Warwickshire v Glamorgan	Swansea	1990
203*	Warwickshire v Surrey	Guildford	1994
200*	Griqualand West v Northern Transvaal B	Kimberley	1988
176	Warwickshire v Middlesex	Lord's	1996
174	Griqualand West v Northern Transvaal B	Kimberley	1987
168	Warwickshire v Hampshire	Southampton	1997
164	Warwickshire v Northamptonshire	Northampton	1996
151	Warwickshire v Kent	Edgbaston	1987

CENTURIES IN ONE-DAY CRICKET

127	Warwickshire v Buckinghamshire	Edgbaston	1987
105*	Warwickshire v Kent	Edgbaston	1994

15,000 FIRST-CLASS RUNS AT AN AVERAGE OF 40
England-qualified batsmen who did not play Test cricket

P.D. Bowler	19,567 @ 40.51
J.C. Hildreth	18,000 @ 41.00
A.D. Brown	16,898 @ 42.67
A.J. Moles	15,305 @ 40.70

A.D. Brown played one-day internationals for England

TROPHIES WON WITH WARWICKSHIRE

County Championship	1994, 1995
NatWest Trophy	1989, 1993, 1995
Benson & Hedges Cup	1994
Sunday League	1994

COACHING APPOINTMENTS

Gill College, Eastern Cape, South Africa

St George's School, Buenos Aires

Free State, South Africa

Hong Kong

Kenya

Scotland

England Under-19

Northern Districts, New Zealand

New Zealand

University of Western Cape, South Africa

South Western Districts, South Africa

Wellingborough School, Northamptonshire

Afghanistan

Afghanistan Under-19

Uzbekistan

Bahamas

INDEX

A
Abberley, Neal 24,28,57
Abdul Qadir 27
Adams, Andre 106
Adams, Jimmy 86,90,109
Agathangelou, Andrea 130
Aldridge, Graeme 106-7
Allott, Geoff 120-1,123
Allott, Paul 30,38,40
Ambrose, Curtly 49,58
Amiss, Dennis 27-8,32-3, 50,56,80,99-100,103
Anurag Singh 75
Arthur, Mickey 41
Asghar Afghan *(Stanikzai)* 135,137,142
Asif Din 28,30,37,44,47,54,75,159
Asim Butt 98
Atherton, Mike 47,52
Atkinson, Ron 69

B
Baartman, Ottniel 130
Bacher, Ali 35
Bailey, Rob 45
Baker, James 111
Bannister, Jack 37-8,46
Baptiste, Eldine 77
Bell, Ian 137
Benjamin, Joey 47
Beukes, Jonathan 97-8
Bicknell, Darren 47
Bicknell, Martin 47
Bird, Dickie 74
Boje, Nicky 83,88,91
Bolton, Paul 99
Bond, Shane 137
Booth, Paul 80
Border, Allan 142
Bosch, Corbin 42
Bosch, Eathan 42
Bosch, Karen-Anne 42

Bosch, Tertius 42
Botham, Ian 21,43-4,75
Bracewell, John 109,111-2,125
Bradman, Don 58
Brown, David 11,27,31-2,35,37-8
Brown, Dougie 98,102
Buchanan, John 111
Burl, Ryan 139
Burns, Mike 74

C
Callaghan, James 23
Capel, David 57
Carter, Neil 97
Chase, Dick 24-5
Cheslin, Mike 24
Chopra, Varun 104
Claughton, John 99
Collingwood, Paul 117-8
Cottam, Bob 46,72,88,101,103
Cowdrey, Chris 78
Cronje, Ewie 91
Cronje, Hansie 83-7,90-1
Currie, Dave 119-20,124-5
Curtis, Tim 61

D
Davis, Dickie 78
Davis, Mark 32
Dawlat Zadran 137,141
Dean, Geoffrey 16
DeFreitas, Phil 40
Delport, Cameron 139-40
Dilley, Graham 43-4
Dippenaar, Boeta 83,87
Donald, Allan 34-6,39-40,51-3,62,68, 70,74,77-9,81,83-4,87,91
Donald, Tina 35,62,84
Done, Richard 101-2

Drinnen, Peter 103,136

E
Ellcock, Ricardo 31
Elliott, Grant 118
Elworthy, Steve 41
Emburey, John 60,76-7
Emrit, Rayad 139
Evans, Alun 106

F
Farrelly, Mark 169
Farrelly, Megan 128,152-5,157,169
Feltham, Mark 44
Ferreira, Anton 25,33,42,82
Finch, Aaron 137
Finch, Tony 11,17-8,99,155
Finn, Steven 103
Fletcher, Stuart 78
Flynn, Daniel 111
Fowler, Graeme 40
Freeman, Mark 13,121

G
Gambier, Gautham 116
Gardner, Fred 23
Garner, Joel 32
Gatting, Mike 75-7
Gayle, Chris 113
Getty, Paul 102
Ghai, Sharad 92-4
Gifford, Norman 27-9,31,33,38-9,73,77
Giles, Ashley 159-60
Gooch, Graham 38,45,47
Gough, Darren 49
Gould, Ian 35
Gower, David 45,75
Graveney, David 33,155
Greatbatch, Mark 99-101,123-4
Gupthill, Martin 115

H

Hadlee, Richard	27,117
Hamid Hassan	135-7
Hamilton, Lewis	134
Hamilton-Brown, Rory	103
Hauritz, Nathan	119
Hayhurst, Andy	40
Hick, Graeme	29,61
Hoffman, Paul	97-9
Hoggard, Matthew	87-8
Hollioake, Adam	139
Holloway, Pieran	39
Hooper, Carl	74
Houghton, Neil	99-100
Hughes, Simon	44
Humpage, Geoff	11,27,30-1,37,40,47,81
Humphries, Dave	31

I

Ikram Alikhil	140
Illingworth, Ray	65
Imran Khan	73-4,142
Inverarity, John	97
Inzamam-ul-Haq	138

J

Jackson, Michael	154
James, Kevan	31
Jayawardene, Mahela	135
Jennings, Keaton	87
Jennings, Ray	87
Johnson, Mitchell	137
Jones, Adrian	70
Jones, Dean	140
Joyce, Ed	98-9

K

Kabir Khan	134
Kallicharran, Alvin	29,33,44
Kirsten, Gary	116,118
Klusener, Lance	141,152
Knight, Nick	65,67,72,83
Kock, Nic	129
Kohli, Virat	104
Kumble, Anil	68

L

Lamb, Allan	37,68,75
Lane, Mark	95,101
Lara, Brian	56-66
Larkins, Wayne	45
Lawrence, David	33
Leatherdale, David	75
Le Roux, Garth	35
Lloyd, Andy	17,27,31-3,39,71-2,108
Lloyd, Clive	30,32
Lloyds, Jeremy	33
Lord, Gordon	24,27-9,43,48,82
Lusardi, Seppi	91
Lyth, Adam	103

M

McCauley, Ray	86
McCosh, Donald	41-2
McCullum, Brendon	110-5,117-9,121,123-5,137
McCullum, Nathan	114
McDowell, Jamie	99
Machan, Matt	136
MacIntosh, Tim	111
MacMillan, Brian	24,28,32
Makinson, David	30
Malcolm, Devon	60
Mallender, Neil	70
Mandela, Nelson	83
Marks, Vic	39
Marshall, Hamish	105-6
Marshall, James	54,105,109
Marshall, Malcolm	31-2,39,49,72,74
Mathews, Angelo	135
Medlycott, Keith	47
Merrick, Tony	38
Mills, Kyle	111,115,123
Mohammad Nabi	19
Moles, Danny	46,88,169
Moles, Gill (mother)	21-3,131
Moles, Jacqui	37-9,41,46,55,84,131,169
Moles, Mark	21-2,131,149
Moles, Matthew	55,88,169
Moles, Paul	21-2,158-9
Moles, Simon	21-2
Moles, Stuart (father)	21-2,26,141
Moeen Ali	103-4
Mohammad Shahzad	138
Moody, Tom	51
Morgan, Eoin	98-9,101
Morris, Hugh	47,104
Morris, John	41-2
Mott, Matthew	110,114
Moxon, Martyn	68
Mudassar Nazar	95
Mujeeb Zadran	140
Munton, Sonia	11
Munton, Tim	11-16,44,46-7,51,58-60,64,68,72-3,75,78,99-100,105-6,121,155,159
Muralitharan, Mutthiah	117
Murphy, Tony	32
Mushtaq Ahmed	67

N

Nancy (Lord's cook)	76
Nash, Dion	111
Nasimullah Danish	138
Naveen-ul-Haq	140,144
Neal, Phil	69
Neale, Phil	29
Nel, Andre	87
Nicholas, Mark	32,52,65
Nosworthy, Dave	105-6

O

Oakman, Alan	28,75
O'Brien, Kevin	142
Obuya, Collins	96
O'Donnell, Mark	107-8,118,123-5
Odumbe, Maurice	92-3

Oliver, Keith	102	
Oram, Jacob	111,115,117,123	
Ostler, Dominic	59,61-2,75	

P

Papps, Michael	105
Parsons, Gordon	34,86
Parsons, Hester	86
Patel, Dipak	29
Patel, Jeetan	119,124
Patterson, Patrick	30,32,49
Penney, Trevor	65
Perera, Thisara	135
Pick, Andy	103,167
Pienaar, Roy	35
Pierson, Adrian	52
Pigott, Tony	54
Piper, Keith	52,60,65,72-3
Pollock, Graeme	91
Pollock, Shaun	36
Potter, Laurie	34
Prabakhar, Manoj	56
Pretorius, Dewald	87
Pretorius, Nico	88

R

Rajput, Lalchand	143
Randall, Charles	79
Rashid, Adil	103-4
Rashid Khan	141-2
Ratcliffe, Jason	47,54,76-7
Reeve, Dermot	44,46,51,54-9, 61,63,65,68,72,79,105,113
Rhodes, Jonty	88
Rhodes, Steve	29
Richards, Viv	32
Richardson, Bryan	27
Robinson, Charlie	91
Robinson, Mark	78-9
Ryder, Jesse	111,114-7,119

S

Samiullah Shenwari	135
Sererami, Emanuel	129
Shafiqullah Stanikzai	149
Shapoor Zadran	135-6
Sharafuddin Ashraf	138
Sibanda, Vusi	139
Sidebottom, Ryan	118
Sikander Raza	139
Simmons, Phil	141
Small, Gladstone	9-11,38,51,53,55,63, 65,70,75,81,99,159
Smith, David	25
Smith, David (Sussex)	55
Smith, MJK	56
Smith, Neil	44
Smith, Paul	32-3,38,54,56,59,72,78
Smith, Robin	32
Smith, Roddy	99,101-3
Soumya Sarkar	142
Speak, Nick	40
Steele, David	67
Stephenson, Franklyn	54-5
Stewart, Alec	47
Stewart, Micky	48,65,67
Stewart, Shanan	105
Stovold, Andy	30
Strauss, Andrew	126-7
Strauss, Ruth	127
Stuurman, Glenton	130

T

Taylor, Greg	167-8
Taylor, Paul	75
Taylor, Ross	113
Tendulkar, Sachin	116
Thomas, Bernard	37
Thorne, David	40,80
Tikolo, Steve	93-4
Topley, Don	38,51
Towner, Rob	121-2
Tuffey, Daryl	117
Tufnell, Phil	76-7
Turner, Arthur	128
Turner, Glenn	117
Twose, Roger	54,56,58-9, 61-2,65,70-2

U

Underwood, Derek	77-8
Upton, Paddy	118

V

van den Heever, Brand	162-3
van der Wath, Johan	87
van Wyk, Morne	87,139
van Zyl, Corrie	87,90
Vaughan, Justin	110-2,115,120,122
Vaughan, Michael	68
Vettori, Daniel	111-3,117-20,122-5,137

W

Wais Barmak	140
Walker, Alan	39
Walsh, Courtney	31,33,49,74-5
Waqar Younis	47,49
Wardlaw, Iain	136
Warne, Shane	60
Warner, David	137
Wasim Akram	38-40,74
Wasim Khan	47,88-9
Watkins, Alan	23
Watkinson, Mike	38
Watling, BJ	109
Watson, Ryan	98-9
Whitaker, James	99
Whittall, Guy	56
Willey, Peter	67,70-1
Williamson, Kane	108-9,127
Willis, Bob	42
Windows, Matt	74
Winspear, John	99-100
Woolmer, Bob	51-4,57,63-5,72-3, 82-4,90,92,101,106
Wright, Craig	99,101-3
Wright, John	117,124-5

Y

Yasir Arafat	97